*This book is dedicated to the countless committed couples
who have come in and out of our lives and blessed us
with their example, experience, and encouragement.
You have left a legacy for us.
We hope to do the same for others.*

*And to every couple who picks up this book and is committed
to going the distance for the sake of our Lord Jesus Christ:
We look forward to completing the journey with you.*

ACKNOWLEDGMENTS

Our heartfelt thanks to:

- Our beautiful daughter, Dana. All we do is first for God, and then for you. May you reap the blessings of parents who loved each other and experienced God's grace daily.

- Uncle Owen and Aunt Alice—your legacy has touched our lives and will, prayerfully, now touch many more.

- Our faithful friends (and awesome couples) in ministry who provided rich examples for this book: Dick and Shirley Caldwell, Dan and Chris Castillero, Bob and Mary Beth Maass, Guy and Allison Martin, Dan and Debbie Olson, Steve and Sophie Olson, Kurt and Sara Staeuble, Alex and Mitzi Steele, Steve and Rhonda Stoppe, Don and Barbara Willett, and Lance and Pam Workman.

- Our "family" at Harvest House Publishers for believing in us for yet another book.

And above all, we are grateful to our Lord and Savior, Jesus Christ, who makes *all* things possible.

WHEN COUPLES WALK TOGETHER

CINDI & HUGH MCMENAMIN

HARVEST HOUSE PUBLISHERS

EUGENE, OREGON

Cover by Left Coast Design, Portland, Oregon

Cover photo © Yuri Arcurs / Shutterstock; Backcover author photo by Karlyn Dagraedt © Savvy Snaps Photography

WHEN COUPLES WALK TOGETHER
Copyright © 2010 by Cindi McMenamin and Hugh McMenamin
Published by Harvest House Publishers
Eugene, Oregon 97402
www.harvesthousepublishers.com

Library of Congress Cataloging-in-Publication Data

McMenamin, Cindi, 1965-
    When couples walk together / Cindi McMenamin and Hugh McMenamin.
        p. cm.
    ISBN 978-0-7369-2947-9 (pbk.)
    1. Spouses—Prayers and devotions. 2. Marriage—Religious aspects—Christianity—Meditations.
I. McMenamin, Hugh. II. Title.
    BV4596.M3M448 2010
    242'.644—dc22
                                                                              2010028731

10 11 12 13 14 15 16 17 / LB-NI / 10 9 8 7 6 5 4 3 2 1

Contents

Introduction: Isn't It Time to Start Walking *Together*?

Do you remember what it was like when you first fell in love? Admit it—you had the picture-perfect idea of what your relationship would be like. You'd do everything together. Life would play out like a fairy tale (or, as Hugh would say, an adventure). You'd understand each other and roll through the situations that trip up most other couples. And then...reality set in. You realized you are two people who are a lot more different from each other than you originally thought. Two people desperately trying to figure out how to do life together.

For years, we were just like that. We were two people who, in some ways, walked alone in our marriage. We never intended for it to be that way. That's just the way it was. Sure, we lived in the same house, slept in the same bed, spent nearly every Friday of our married life together on a "date day." We even raised a daughter, although I wouldn't necessarily say we were good at raising her "together." Hugh did his part. I did mine. And that's the way it was.

I (Cindi) was independent, yet needy (if you can imagine that). I kept telling Hugh I wanted him to be a close part of my life (and I really did), but I wasn't really living like it. I continued to do things my way, and was unintentionally pushing him further away. And I (Hugh), a born introvert, was used to doing things on my own and alone. I knew what marriage was supposed to be all about—two people living as one—but in a lot of areas I continued to operate solo.

Both of us had no idea how to give up our own ambitions, expectations, and conveniences in order to really walk *together*.

But then we started doing some really simple things to change that—things we wish we'd done years ago—and they had a profound effect on our marriage.

This book is for every couple who knows they have potential but aren't living it to the fullest. It's for every couple who wants to draw closer to each other but doesn't know how. It's for young couples starting out and not wanting to make the mistakes most couples make... and it's for seasoned couples who are going the distance and want to take advantage of another resource to help them get there.

This book is not a counseling manual. And it's not filled with fluff (Hugh will personally see to that!). And ladies, it's not an attempt to bang your husband over the head and make him wake up and get a clue as to what you need. It's simply a book to encourage you, motivate you, and even excite you to draw closer to each other because of the wonderful benefits of intimacy, oneness, companionship, and unselfish love. Because you two at one time really enjoyed being together and you might've forgotten just how much. Because life is short and what you waste away now you can never get back.

And men, if you're the kind who has to be dragged, bribed, or made to feel guilty before you'll read a devotional with your wife, relax. I (Hugh) know exactly where you're coming from. This is not a warm and fuzzy piece on how to make your wife happy or a counseling program on "The 31 Things You're Doing Wrong." Rather, think of it as a user's guide to your wife's heart that will unleash some passions in her and get you in touch with some of your own that you didn't know were there (translate: that will press your wife's buttons and will ultimately make you as happy as her). It is our hope and prayer that you'll both enjoy reading through this book *together*.

In every chapter we have a section called "Taking the Next Step." This is where we give some practical advice on how to start walking together. Often this comes down to simply taking the next step. We've tried to cover areas in which we've often found ourselves standing still and we've had to swallow our pride, put self on the line, and with an eye toward a closer connection, take the next step toward walking together.

At the end of each chapter is a section called "Going the Extra Mile." Perhaps you are the kind of reader who skips over the application section or saves the questions for some later time. But we encourage you to go the extra mile together by talking through those questions after you finish reading each chapter. These sections will help you to actually start *walking together* instead of just reading about how to do so.

Finally, each chapter closes with "Going the Distance Through Prayer." We strongly believe that if any marriage is to go the distance, prayer must be a part of it. So instead of just learning how to walk together today, you'll also cultivate a habit of prayer that will help you continue to walk together tomorrow and each day thereafter.

So, are you ready to fall back in love? Are you ready to experience a closer connection? Are you ready to quit thinking primarily about you and start thinking about the two of you? We are. So let us share our path with you that we began to walk—a path that finally, after more than 20 years of marriage, had us walking much closer *together*... in 31 days!

—— ❧ Day 1 ❧ ——

Enjoying the Journey

*Always let him lead you, and he will
clear the road for you to follow.*

Proverbs 3:6 cev

Go ahead. Admit it. Your marriage isn't *everything* you expected it
to be, is it? But that's okay. That doesn't mean it can't someday
be what you'd always hoped it would.

We all enter a relationship—or marriage—with a pie-in-the-sky
dream of what it will be like. Then we find we married someone who
was more different from us than we thought. But marriage isn't about
the final destination—the happily ever after with the person of our
dreams. It's about the journey—getting there, walking together, enjoying the adventure en route to our final destination: a true sense of oneness with the other.

We've noticed through the years that walking together as a couple
is a lot like flying together. There are certain things you must do as you
walk aboard that aircraft and commit yourself to the flight, and many
of them are the same things you must do as you walk down the aisle
and commit yourself to one another in marriage.

Like air travel, living life with another person is all about making
adjustments, dealing with delays, realizing you're not in control, and
having to—at times—make the best of it so you truly enjoy the journey.

We have been married long enough to be able to say that life with the opposite sex is certainly not predictable or routine. With all the flying we have done, we've learned to laugh at incidents that should be predictable by now (delays, missed connections, lost luggage, annoying seat partners, and so on). Having been married more than 20 years, and having counseled many other couples over that time, we have yet to see a marriage that runs like a routine flight—exactly as planned. I (Cindi) have flown a couple hundred times and have experienced everything from flying into tornadoes (twice), sitting next to celebrities, being stranded on deserted runways, getting routed to another flight because of mechanical difficulties with the plane, or being bumped up to first class because of overcrowding. And Hugh and I believe that marriage, too, is full of inconveniences, storms, unexpected bumps, and unanticipated surprises.

Though I (Hugh) have not flown as frequently as Cindi, I've flown several very long-distance flights—into the remote jungles of Papua New Guinea; to the interior of South America; across the diverse regions of Turkey, Israel and Jordan; and through the urban and suburban landscapes of Colombia. And I, too, have seen that marriage, like air travel, can be as enjoyable or as miserable as we choose to see it. Unlike flying to a destination, marriage is all about the journey—the everyday inconveniences that can irritate you, the interesting things you experience en route, the laughs you share that break up the monotony, and the setbacks that occur along the way that can drive you apart or draw you closer to one another.

In spite of unexpected delays (when it comes to having children, buying a house, or achieving a dream), missed flights (or promotions or vacations), and unexpected turbulence (who expects those bumps and dips in marriage, anyway?), marriage *can* be a wonderful trip if you're prepared and you go with the flow. And just as we don't try to jump off an airplane when there's a problem (that would be suicide) we should remain committed to staying on board when it comes to the God-ordained union of marriage. So if you long for your marriage to be a pleasant experience (and who doesn't?) and you want to enjoy the trip (and marriage *is* a trip, alright!), then buckle up, pay attention to the emergency instructions, and sit back and enjoy the flight. Marriage, like an airplane, is not an end in itself but a vehicle through which you arrive at your final destination: a greater sense of oneness.

Taking the Next Step

So here you are in your journey. Whether you are engaged to be married and just starting out, or looking for something to recharge the batteries after a long haul together, it's never too early or too late to set some guidelines to make sure you enjoy the journey. Here are some that we've learned through the years:

1. Realize You Don't Know It All

To enter marriage thinking you know all there is to know about it is like getting on board the aircraft and immediately tuning out the flight attendant who is going over that information which, in case of an emergency, just might save your life. Let's admit it: We would rather start thumbing through the in-flight magazine or try firing off one last text message, thinking *I've heard all this before and I already know what to do.* Really? So try and explain to your spouse right now how to open the emergency exit door or what to do with that inflatable life vest. We think you get our point: Most of us think we are all set to fly smoothly through married life when, in reality, the future is a very big unknown and there's some lifesaving information we had better pay attention to. Do you know where you're headed? Do you have a survival plan if something goes wrong? Are you prepared for the storm that may hit? Turbulence is inevitable in the air and in your marriage. Hopefully your desire is to prepare yourself with survival tips that will help you to persevere through the sudden storms that come your way.

2. Expect the Unexpected

Like every flight, every marriage is unique. You will encounter your own share of storms, delays, inconveniences, and downright disasters. But how you get through them makes all the difference. The unexpected (be it unmet expectations or a full-blown crisis!) can pull a couple apart or draw them closer together. If you go through life realizing that storms may come, you will weather them better. Airplanes are now built with de-icers that help warm the wings and prevent ice buildup. Through this book we hope to provide de-icers for your marriage that will help warm things up when conditions start getting cold.

3. Remember You're in It for the Long Haul

The marriage relationship is designed to be forever. The problem is that we live in a society that doesn't know what *forever* means anymore. Hopefully, your vows were the traditional ones that had meaning to them: "for better or for worse, in sickness and in health, till death do us part." That's a long time for most of us. That means forever…while we're on this earth.

Knowing that you and your spouse are committed until your dying day will save you from some disasters that might seem bigger than they really are. There were times, early in our marriage, when Cindi would fear that it was over (or I didn't love her anymore) because I (Hugh) was upset over something that had nothing at all to do with her. I would have to remind her that my "till death do us part" was sincere and I wasn't planning on either of us dying anytime soon!

When you're on an airplane, you can't get up in the middle of the trip and demand that the pilot turn the airplane around or tell him to land in a different location. (Yikes! They arrest people for stuff like that!) You're committed for the duration of the flight—in the face of bad company, turbulence, little leg room, bad food (or in some cases no food), and whatever else happens. Realizing that you're in your marriage for the long haul will help when you find yourself in the panic mode.

4. Receive Help Along the Way

Once you board a flight, you are putting your trip—and very life—into the hands of a skilled, capable pilot. Whether you acknowledge personal trust or confidence in the pilot or not, he or she is still the one who will take you where you need to go. In addition, the airplane is staffed with skilled flight attendants who know far more about flying than you do. Similarly, when it comes to your marriage, your relationship is in God's hands, whether you realize it or not. He's the Pilot and He knows where you're going and He is the only one who can get you there. In addition, He has strategically placed certain skilled couples or individuals in your life who may know more about marriage than you and your spouse. Take advantage of their experience. Heed their advice when it comes to whatever might make your trip more enjoyable. Be willing to accept help and even ask for it when you need it. They, too, want your journey to be an enjoyable and successful one. It's these kinds of people—your pastor, your friends, your parents, a mentor couple in your church, that couple who is evidently so "in love" after all these years—whom you need to turn to and ask for assistance. There's a reason they are on the same journey that you are taking and headed in the same direction.

5. Invest in Some In-flight (or Midlife!) Entertainment

Some flights are long and boring and marriage is a long flight, literally. It will (prayerfully) last the rest of your life. How do you keep yourself from becoming agitated, cramped up, and downright miserable with your mate and others around you? You don't just jump out the window or emergency exit when you're bored or pick up with a cute flight attendant. Remember why you're on the flight, whom you're with, and where it is you're going. You'll have a much better time en route if you stay pleasant toward each other. This means keeping things fresh all through your marriage. Take that overseas trip you've always dreamed of taking together (before you're both too old to enjoy it). Invest in a date night once a week to catch up with each other and keep the relationship alive. Go ahead and pay for a night in that expensive hotel as an investment in the two of you and a way to break up the monotony of life. Get those amusement park passes for a pick-me-up when it's been awhile since the two of you have been able to have child-like fun with one another. In this book, we will provide for you some ideas for "in-flight entertainment" on your journey through marriage.

6. Handle the Takeoffs and Landings Carefully

The two most dangerous parts of any airline flight are the takeoff and the landing. And how well you get started and how well you finish are also the two most crucial steps in a marriage. If for some reason you think it seems too late to "start well," remember that the beauty of marriage is that every day can be a fresh start. Every morning, as you greet your husband or wife with a hug or kiss, you can determine to provide a good takeoff for you and your spouse. And every night, as you fall off to sleep together—or touch base on the phone if you're apart—you can do whatever you know will help ensure a good landing. We want to help you get off to a good start (if you're reading this together in the morning) or enjoy a good landing (if you choose to read this together before saying goodnight).

Remember, it's the choices you make each day during the sometimes monotonous stretches of your marriage flight that contribute to the success of the journey. Enjoy the journey—you both know it's worth it!

—— Going the Extra Mile ——

Spend a few minutes discussing the following questions with one another. Our hope is that doing this will draw you closer together and help you experience a better takeoff or landing today.

1. What are some things about your life together that you truly love?

2. What are some of the good things that you two share that you never anticipated before your marriage?

3. Imagine taking a trip together. What important steps can you take along the way to ensure that you two experience a good time together? (Be creative here!)

4. How can you apply your answers to question 3 to your life and marriage so you truly enjoy the journey?

5. Read the following verses of Scripture and record the insights each offers as guidance for your journey:

Proverbs 3:5-6:

Philippians 2:1-2:

Ephesians 4:32:

Colossians 3:12-14:

——Going the Distance Through Prayer——

God, You have blessed us with an opportunity to share our lives together. Let us never take that opportunity for granted. Let us never forget that it's a privilege to be in a relationship with another person who has committed their life to us. Every time we see a person going through life alone, may we be reminded to be thankful that we have a partner to accompany us on this journey.

Lord, in the same way, don't let us take for granted the times when we enjoy blue skies and smooth sailing. Every day we have together is a gift because life is a gift. And love—through the spouse you've given each of us—is a gift, too. When we hit some bumps and swings along the way, help us to realize they are only temporary. Please keep our hearts focused on the few things that matter—enjoying the journey and showing grace to each other along the way. Thank You that, in the same way You will not desert us in this journey called life, You will give us—as we ask for Your help—the staying power to not desert each other. We hold onto the promise that You are with us on this adventure called life. May it truly be a grand adventure. And may we enjoy every step of the journey—together.

Leaving Self on the Shelf

*Each of you should look not only to your own
interests, but also to the interests of others.*

PHILIPPIANS 2:4

I (Cindi) remember the day marriage finally made sense to me. I was flying to a speaking engagement and complaining to the Lord in prayer: *God, You knew what I was like and what I would need in a husband. So are You sure You knew what You were doing when You led me to Hugh?*

I was convinced God had brought the two of us together. I knew He was in it from the day I met Hugh. But certainly God also knew that my husband would not be one to express himself verbally in the way I was expecting. Certainly God knew that I would many times need more emotional support than my husband appeared able to give. So why did God let us get married? And why wasn't He transforming my husband to become the kind of man who would meet my needs and expectations?

While those thoughts were going through my mind, suddenly I felt as if God had pulled me aside and whispered something profound to me: "Perhaps I was looking at what *he* needed."

According to the Bible, man was created in the image of God. And woman was created to be man's helper. Woman was created so man would be *complete*. God didn't create Adam so Eve could just be romanced. To the contrary, He created Eve so Adam would have a helper—one suited for him in every way.[1]

In other words, it wasn't all about *me*. Ouch!

I'm embarrassed to say that for the first 15 or so years of our marriage, I never really thought too much about what my husband needed in a wife. Instead, I thought quite a bit about what I needed in a husband and how Hugh was falling short of my expectations. I hadn't put my own feelings aside long enough to say, "God, show me why You brought me into this man's life and how I can truly help him be all that You created him to be." I hadn't put myself on the shelf long enough to see the bigger, more beautiful picture of what God has in mind when He brings two people, who are very different from each other, together to form a union.

It's tough to leave self on the shelf. Self wants to rule. Self wants its own way. Self suffocates. And self destroys.

The Bible shows us what the opposite of self looks like when it describes love, which is selfless:

> Love is kind and patient, never jealous, boastful, proud, or rude. Love isn't selfish or quick tempered. It doesn't keep a record of wrongs that others do. Love rejoices in the truth, but not in evil. Love is always supportive, loyal, hopeful, and trusting. Love never fails! (1 Corinthians 13:4-8 CEV).

Sometimes our marriage looks the opposite of the biblical description of love. We can act unkind, impatient, jealous, boastful, proud, and even rude! There are times we are quick-tempered with each other. And God knows there are times we keep records of the wrongs we do to each other. But recognizing what we *don't* want our relationship to look like is one of the first steps to walking together toward a newer, fresher, lovelier one.

When I arrived home from that speaking engagement, I had a new perspective on my marriage. Instead of praying for my husband to meet *my* needs, I began to ask God to show me how I could meet my *husband's*. Instead of looking at *his* shortcomings, I began to ask God to expose to me my own. Instead of focusing on my desires, I began to pray about how I could meet his. And this new outlook not only gave me grace to extend to Hugh's weaknesses (as I became more aware of my own), it also changed my heart. And our marriage.

Now I (Hugh) would like to offer my perspective on this. It's a pretty tough load to bear when your wife is expecting you to meet all her emotional needs. Yes, we want our wives to admire and look up to us, but we don't want them to turn us into a god in their lives. That's a bill we could never fill. But there are moments when I unreasonably expect *her* to make me happy—by assuming she will understand what I'm going through by being able to read my mind, or by expecting her to be there for whatever I happen to need. And then there are other moments I put myself first when I've had a rough day and I expect Cindi to cater to me. Or, because I'm the head of the house, priest of the family, lord of the manor, king of the castle (guys, insert your favorite phrase of entitlement here), I tend to think my personal demands have priority over everyone else's under my roof. But it's vital that we husbands *not* place a burden on our wives that we wouldn't want them to place on us.

Our friend, Rhonda, sums up how she was able to leave herself on the shelf in her marriage when it came to expecting her husband, Steve, to meet all her needs: "As I grew more intimate with Christ, I let my husband off the hook. He no longer had to be my *everything*. I could find joy, rest, security and peace in my relationship with Christ. My husband no longer had to be my god. He could be my husband, my friend, my ministry mate. The intimacy in our relationship has always been healthier when I pursue intimacy with Christ first over trying to squeeze every ounce of life out of my husband to make me *feel* like we are intimate. As we each work on growing more intimate with Christ, we find we are more intimate with each other."

Women are not the only ones who need to take their primary needs to God in the relationship. If a husband is expecting his wife to be his all in all, he, too, will be disappointed. She can only give so much. He must look to God, his heavenly Father, for his affirmation, sense of worth, and validation as a man. As he becomes certain of who he is in God's eyes, he won't depend on his wife to fill a hole in his soul.

In their book *Love and War*, John and Stasi Eldredge contend that marriage is a "divine conspiracy." It's God's "workshop" to transform our lives, they say. "God is going to use your marriage to get to issues in your life he wants to address."[2] We agree. Marriage is tough. It shows us how selfish we tend to be. It shows us how much we need God to mend the brokenness in our lives. It shows us how far we really need to go when it comes to being Christlike in our individual lives and in our marriage. But when we get a glimpse of what God wants to do in and through each of us to help us become more like Himself, we find we have an awesome privilege and responsibility in front of us in this arena called marriage.

Taking the Next Step

To be part of God's workshop in another's life is to say, "God, not what I need, but what my spouse needs. Use me to build up and encourage my spouse and make him [or her] the person You want them to be." When we say, "Not what I need, but what my spouse needs," we are, in a sense, imitating the prayer Jesus uttered before He went to the cross, in which He said to His Father, "Not My will, but Yours, be done."[3] Jesus was literally giving up His life for ours. So can we, then, be willing to give up our own comforts, needs, and expectations for the other?

There is no more direct way to draw your spouse's heart toward yours than to put yourself on the shelf and say, "Not my will, but yours."

- Not my choice of a restaurant tonight, but yours.
- Not my choice of a movie this time, but yours.
- Not my night to have uninterrupted sleep, but yours.
- Not my story to dominate the conversation, but yours.
- Not my feelings to protect today, but yours.
- Not my dream to pursue right now, but yours.

As you develop a habit of putting the other person first, you may be surprised to find that the phrase eventually becomes "Not my _____, but *ours*."

Can you leave yourself on the shelf long enough to truly put your husband or wife first? Such selflessness doesn't come naturally. At times, it doesn't come easy. But it does bring priceless—and precious—results. You will end up drawing your hearts closer together.

Start walking together today by leaving yourself on the shelf.

——Going the Extra Mile——

Hugh here: All right, guys—you can either stop here because you're convinced by this point you've got the basics. Or you can admit that this marriage thing is a bit more complex than you imagined and take it the extra step. Go over these questions with your wife and let them draw you both into a closer connection.

1. Can you recall a time when you gave up something you really wanted and you ended up being happier because you did something the two of you could do together?

2. Tell your spouse a tangible way that you can leave yourself on the shelf this week so you can put him/her first.

3. Now ask your spouse to tell you, lovingly, how you can put yourself second this week as a way of showing your spouse that he/she is first.

4. Look up the following verses and write them out in your own words. How does each relate to putting yourself on the shelf?

    1 Corinthians 13:4-5— Love is about what you do, not about you.

Philippians 2:3-4— *Put others above yourself.*

Philippians 2:5-8— *Have the mind + heart of Jesus Serving others*

1 Peter 5:6-7— *Submit your will to God.*

——Going the Distance Through Prayer——

Pray through this version of the Bible's "love passage" (1 Corinthians 13:4-8) together as a way of reminding each other how to put the other person first:

> Lord, You know that we truly desire to love each other as You have loved us. So, please help us to become people who never give up on each other. Help us care more for each other than we do for ourselves. Help each of us not to want what we don't have, but to cherish what we do have. Don't let our individual pride get in the way of our oneness. Keep us each from forcing ourselves on the other in order to get our own way. Don't let "Me first!" enter into either of our minds or our vocabularies, but instead help us to have a "You first" mentality.
>
> Lord, help us to not fly off the handle with each other, keep score of one another's wrongs, or revel when the other grovels. Help us, instead, to take pleasure in the truth. God, give us the strength to put up with anything, trust You always, continually look for the best in one another, and never look back. Keep us walking together to the end.[4]

From Tense to Tender

*A kind answer soothes angry feelings, but
harsh words stir them up.*

PROVERBS 15:1 CEV

Hugh was ticking me off.

I didn't realize that when he opened the restaurant door for me and I walked in, he didn't want me going straight to the restaurant hostess and "taking charge" by telling her there were two of us for dinner. What's so wrong with that? Then as we were being escorted into the "loud room" at one of our favorite restaurants, I asked if we could instead sit in a booth we had just passed, located in a quieter section. As the hostess walked us to the booth and laid the menus on the table, Hugh tossed his phone and keys onto the table and sat down with somewhat of a scowl.

Great! I thought sarcastically. *We're in for a lovely evening.* I asked him what I had done wrong. (Not a good question to start off with, by the way.)

"Can you let me lead once in a while?" he asked curtly. I sat there like I'd been hit in the face. I wasn't aware that I had offended him by taking charge of things as soon as we had walked into the restaurant. I looked down. I wanted to cry. *I don't want to be here,* I thought. *I want to leave right now and walk home.* My expectations for the evening weren't panning out.

Neither were Hugh's.

I (Hugh) had wanted the evening to be a date during which I treated my wife to a night out. You guys know what I'm talking about: the make-the-reservations, pull-out-her-chair, order-for-her kind of night. So Cindi wasn't the only one disappointed. She was being a little too controlling for my taste. I didn't need her to have everything "in hand" or taken care of—that's what I wanted to be for her that night, and I felt that being taken away at her every move.

For a moment, both of us were thinking, *This stinks.* The tension was high. I (Cindi) panicked for a minute. *How do we get something so stupid to just dissolve so we can redeem the evening?* I opted to be quiet for a while. Sometimes the less I say, the better, especially when I'm feeling wounded.

Thank God Hugh was the bigger person that night. He took a few deep breaths (careful to not make them sound like exasperated sighs, of course) and asked me what looked good on the menu.

"I know," he said. "Let's both try something we've never had before. Let's make this an adventure."

To be honest, the only adventure I wanted at that moment was to show him what it *really* looks like when his wife takes charge. I wanted to give him the adventure of a nice meal to himself! But the fact that he instantly became a young boy ("Let's both try something we've never done before") and the fact that he was trying to redeem the evening got to me. Eventually I softened up. I ordered the Burrito Gigantic, he got the Carnitas Quesadilla, and we truly enjoyed the rest of the evening.

How do you redeem the moment when it looks like everything is quickly going downhill? How do you recover from a stinging comment or a rude response? How do you forget about the little irritations that make you feel that you've finally really had it? By showing grace, realizing you do the same things to your spouse that you accuse him or her of doing to you, and becoming tender.

Taking the Next Step

So when you're in the midst of the irritation (or the heat of the battle, whichever applies), neither one of you wants to make the first move. That would be like admitting *you* were at fault. But look at it this way: Making the first move is basically being the bigger person... and reaching out in love. And as Scripture says, love never fails.[5] That's why it's so important that one of you reach out. And *you* can be the bigger person. Whatever it is that irritated you isn't worth flushing the evening down the toilet. So, when the tension starts rising, try one of these tender gestures:

- An inside joke or something just the two of you share. It's a connection point to make you realize that underneath your irritation, you are best of friends.

- Touch can help tone down the tension. Reach out and touch the other person's hand. Or, like we do, offer the other person your pinky finger. That's like saying, "I know you don't feel like holding my hand right now, but will you take *just my finger?*" It's humbling. And your spouse might need that. When Hugh does that, it softens me every time.

- Make your spouse laugh. Hugh will pull a geek face on me and it never fails to make me smile.

Looking back now, in all fairness, it was the dinner hour at the end of a full day and we were each probably just as hungry and grumpy as the other. When tensions arise, giving the other person the benefit of the doubt might help pull the two of you closer together. Try offering a tender touch on the hand or shoulder, or just flat out admitting you were wrong. Love covers a multitude of sins.

——Going the Extra Mile——

Now, to make sure you two don't blow your next evening out, talk with each other about the following (knowing the answers to these questions may be your key to a closer connection):

1. What things beyond our control can inadvertently add tension to our evenings?

2. What is one thing you need from me that would turn the tension into a tender moment?

3. What is one thing I should *not* do when the evening starts getting tense?

——Going the Distance Through Prayer——

Lord Jesus, thank You that You lived life on this earth and therefore, You understand that tension is a part of this life. Thank You that because You have experienced life's difficulties, You can help us overcome what seeks to overwhelm and conquer us. Help us rise above those tense moments that could lead us to say hurtful things to each other. Help us realize that learning to connect with each other when we might not feel like it moves us one step closer to understanding Your unconditional love for us. Give each of us the discernment to know when to say something sweet or give a loving touch or just reach out in kindness so the other knows we want to redeem the moment and start over if that's the best course of action. May we learn, during the tense and trying moments in life, to be more like You in every way.

— DAY 4 —

Praising the Positive

*Don't ever stop thinking about what is truly
worthwhile and worthy of praise.*

PHILIPPIANS 4:8 CEV

When I started dating Hugh, my youth pastor—a longtime friend of Hugh's—pulled me aside and felt he needed to warn me. "Cindi, Hugh is an awesome guy, and I'd highly recommend him as a husband, but he's also the moodiest person I know."

"Hugh's *not* moody," I responded defensively. "He's a deep thinker. He takes a while to think about things before speaking, instead of just blurting out of his mouth whatever comes to his mind, like I tend to do. I appreciate that about him. That's what I *want* in a husband."

Now, after 22 years of marriage, instead of appreciating my deep thinker, I find myself, at times, thinking things like *Hugh is the moodiest person I know.*

Well, guys (Hugh here), see if you can relate. I loved how my wife was able to express herself back when I first met her. Being a journalism major who wrote beautifully, she could also speak confidently and had a way with words. That's nice when you're getting a love letter or praise and affirmation from a woman in love with you. But after more than 20 years together, there are days when I wish she wasn't quite as verbal, especially when she finds something she thinks is wrong with me. Sometimes, today, when I think about her "way with words" it isn't always in a fond way. She's reciting her thoughts unabridged and I'm looking for the *Reader's Digest* version.

How is it that when we fall in love, the object of our hearts can do no wrong? We overlook their weaknesses or, at times, don't see them at all. Love is blind. And oh how blissful the blind state can be! Then, sometime down the road, the one we fell in love with—the one with all those wonderful character traits—is simply being who he or she is (a deep thinker or one who verbally expresses herself) and is hammered for being annoying, irritating, and difficult to live with.

My, how we need to become blind again—blind to each other's faults, blind to the things that annoy us, blind to bitterness. And open to grace and forgiveness.

There are some who say that the characteristics in your spouse that irritate you today are manifestations of the same characteristics that originally drew you toward each other. What you once found attractive, you now find annoying. We can see that in our marriage, too. I (Cindi) was drawn to Hugh's depth, his seriousness, his contemplative nature. And Hugh was drawn to my confidence, my social skills, and my ability to express myself. Yet those characteristics, after a few years of life together, can grate on our nerves rather than give us a sense of appreciation for each other.

We've learned that we have to pick up a new set of lenses that seeks out and focuses on the positive in each other so we can continue to stay in love. Love, after all, *is* blind. Or, maybe a better way to say it is this: Love *chooses* to be blind to the less flattering traits of one's lover.

In Philippians 4:8 we are told how to keep our minds from focusing on the negative:

> Keep your minds on whatever is true, pure, right, holy, friendly, and proper. Don't ever stop thinking about what is truly worthwhile and worthy of praise (CEV).

That advice works not only in life, but also in marriage, especially when it comes to how you choose to view your spouse. We say *choose* because it *is* a choice. Our fallen human nature tends to notice the negative and focus on it. A divine nature (God's love working through you) will see the best in the other—"the best, not the worst; the beautiful, not the ugly; things to praise, not things to curse" (Philippians 4:8 MSG).

Taking the Next Step

By looking for the good intention, the silver lining, the shred of goodness in something your spouse is doing that annoys you, you will condition yourself to become one who praises the positive in another person.

Here are some ways you can praise the positive in your spouse:

- *She makes you wait by talking too much to other people after church*—Be grateful she is friendly and other people enjoy being around her. How embarrassing if she were someone no one wanted to talk with or be around.

- *He undertipped the server again at your favorite restaurant.* That really bugs you. But you realize his intention was not to insult the server, but to save an extra buck. His prudence, although annoying at times, may help keep you out of debt and allow you to enjoy some things you wouldn't otherwise enjoy. Or maybe, just maybe, he's saving that extra money to spend on *you.*

- *She interrupted you and came across as the one who was in control...again.* That annoys you to no end. But realizing she's a take-charge gal has saved your family in numerous situations in which you weren't there to protect them. For that, give her an extra squeeze and tell her (gently, and at a more appropriate time) how you would've preferred to handle the situation.

There have been times when Hugh clearly did not want to attend a social event that I insisted he accompany me to. Once there, he became lively, interested in the conversations around him, and we truly had a great time. After we arrived home, I made a point of thanking him for accompanying me even though he wasn't thrilled about going, for extending himself to others the way he did, and for not letting his earlier attitude about the event affect my enjoyment of it. I noticed, later, that he was more willing to accompany me to social events after I had praised his efforts and his willingness to do something for me. A little praise goes a long way.

Has it been awhile since you've praised the positive in your better half? Go ahead and make a list of at least five things you appreciate about your spouse, then leave that list somewhere for him or her to see, or read it the next time the two of you have dinner together, or call your spouse once a day for the next five days simply to share with him or her one thing on that list.

You'll be surprised at how praising the positive qualities about each other will draw the two of you closer together.

——Going the Extra Mile——

1. Talk about what drew the two of you toward each other when you were first dating. What characteristics in each other did you especially admire or appreciate?

   His admirable traits: strong love for God + others, generous spirit, funny, adventurous, hottie!

   Her admirable traits: sweet, kind, pretty great w/ kids

2. Now which of those characteristics listed above might be connected to incidents that annoy you about the other person today?

   His:

   Hers:

Admit to your spouse that *you* and *your* perception is what has changed, and ask forgiveness for not seeing him or her in the best light.

3. What do the following verses have to say in relation to praising the positive in your spouse?

    Philippians 4:8—

    Focus on what you love about them.

    Ephesians 4:29—

    Watch what you say!

    James 1:19—

    Think before you react.

4. Choose one of the verses above (you can both agree on the same one, or you can each choose a different one) and copy it onto an index card and put it in a prominent place where each of you (or both of you) will see it and remember to praise the positive in each other.

——Going the Distance Through Prayer——

Lord, You know all about each of us. You know our every weakness, wound, and wart. And yet You choose to love us anyway. And You say gracious things to us in Your Word. You say that Your thoughts of us are precious (Psalm 139:17), that we are white as snow (Isaiah 1:18), that we are Your friend (John 15:15), and that we are chosen (Ephesians 1:4). Help us to learn from that kind of love how to praise the positive in each other. Help us to see "the best, not the worst; the beautiful, not the ugly; things to praise, not things to curse." Give us

Your eyes, Lord Jesus, for one another, so we will speak words that build each other up, not tear each other down. May our love for each other reflect, more and more, Your love for us. Show us how to imitate Your love in how we perceive each other and speak to one another.

The Power of a Note

…my tongue is the pen of a skillful writer.

PSALM 45:1

I was feeling out of sorts on a particular Tuesday. My feelings were hurt about a comment my husband made toward me the night before. My expectations were not met in a conversation with a friend that morning. My daughter sounded ungrateful when I picked her up from school. I responded to her teenage attitude with an immature attitude of my own, which only escalated the situation. I was exasperated. Tensions were rising. And something inside of me was ready to blow.

I walked through the front door in tears, feeling lousy and unloved. Feeling unappreciated and unworthy. Feeling unqualified to do anything at all. I walked up the stairs and into my study—and stopped abruptly! *There* it was…

On my computer keyboard was a single red rose, wrapped in cellophane. On it was a note, in my husband's handwriting, that simply said, "Love you, Wife."

Oh, the power of a note.

I am loved.

I am *not* a loser. I am *loved.*

And in that moment of being reminded I was loved, I was empowered. Everything that went wrong that day dissolved away as my tears of appreciation for the one who expressed love toward me welled up in my eyes and spilled over onto my cheeks. I was no longer feeling desperate…only anxious to express my gratitude to the one who had expressed his love toward me.

It wasn't a huge revelation. Deep down, I knew my husband loved me. But the gesture—right there in front of me—the expression, simple yet sincere, spoke volumes. I was reminded. I was brought back to reality. I am loved.

We all have days that make us want to blow (women probably more than men, I would say!). Stifled anger, stored-up insults, tensions and pressures, hormones and sugar lows. And our inclination is to just blow and get it all out. But that often occurs at the expense of those whom we love the most.

What if, during those difficult days, you could remember something at the core of your being? You are loved. Not just by your spouse, but by the Author of Love, the One who gave Himself for you so that you might live eternally with Him. The God who would rather die than live without you found a way to make you His own.

What if—on those days that your wife is really having a hard time—you found a way to remind her that she is loved? What if—during those times that your man is under extreme pressure and coming up with few words for you—you found some extra meaningful words for him? What if you both realized, in the fiery pit of everyday tensions, the power of a note?

Early in our marriage, Hugh learned just how far the power of a note will go. Because my job requires me to travel quite a bit, there were, and still are, times when my suitcase is constantly in my bedroom. Unpacked one day, and lying empty to be repacked the next. Then it sits there for a few more days, nearly packed, as I prepare to leave again. Hugh learned this was the perfect opportunity to tuck a note or two into my suitcase that I would find after I arrived at my destination. During some trips, he's been rather creative and managed to slip three or four notes in various places that I continued to find throughout my two- or three-day stay. The notes represented simple words of encouragement that he was thinking of me, missing me, and looking forward to my return.

Don and Barbara have discovered the power of a note as well. Sometimes it isn't so much what the note says, but the fact that one of them went the extra step to leave one for the other. "I leave sticky notes on the bathroom mirror when I leave town so he comes home to it," Barbara said. "Also a sticky note on his pillow so when he turns back the covers...voila...he knows I'm thinking about him. That doesn't come from a place of insecurity (I hope he'll think about me while I'm gone) but from a heart that wants to do something special for *him*. Being deliberate and intentional by leaving a note is a selfless, thoughtful act. It is a gift."

Could you cultivate a closer connection with one another by starting to leave simple but powerful notes? Could you be the author of simple words on a sticky note that show the person you love the most how much he or she is on your mind and heart? You don't have to be a poet, and if you accidentally spell a word wrong, you just might endear yourself to his or her heart even more.

Taking the Next Step

Okay, Hugh here, and I know what you're thinking, bro. You don't want to write your wife a mushy letter. But even if you flunked high school English, I know you can accomplish this one. Here are some ideas for simple yet much-appreciated notes for the love of your life:

- You're still the one for me.
- I'm a lucky man to have you.
- You've stolen my heart with a simple glance of your eyes. (Yep, the Song of Songs in the Bible has great lines for you to plagiarize and pass off as your own!)
- You still look hot! (For some reason, that one *never* fails.)
- Can't wait to see you tonight. (Let your wife read into that whatever she wants.)
- I know...I'll prove myself to you. (Okay, sometimes I use lines from movies, like *Ghostbusters*, that we enjoy watching

together. Your notes don't have to mean anything. If they refer to a private joke or something you both share, she'll appreciate it. And you know how we love to make 'em laugh.)

All right ladies (Cindi here), try some of these for him. And don't worry if he reads the following ideas with you. Trust me, he may just forget most of them so they'll still be a surprise when you decide to pull them out and use them on him:

- Write "I love you" on a napkin in the lunch he packed for work (or better yet, you pack the lunch and leave the signed napkin!).
- Put a sticky note on his car dashboard or steering wheel that says, "You drive me crazy…in a good way!"
- What do *you* want to do tonight? (Let him use his imagination as to what you might have had in mind when you wrote that.)
- You're the best.
- Thanks for all your hard work.
- I appreciate all you do.
- You still drive me wild.

Are you getting the idea? We knew you would. This is one of the simplest ways to endear your spouse's heart to yours. Experience a closer connection today through the power of a note.

—— Going the Extra Mile ——

1. Can you recall receiving a note that encouraged you at just the right time? Share the power it had on you.

2. When have you left a note for someone else that encouraged that person at just the right time? How did it make you feel?

3. Share with one another the kinds of words that resonate with your heart and the times at which they would be most appropriate.

4. In the space below, write out some of these love notes recorded in Scripture as ideas for how you can encourage and show your love for one another in a note.

Song of Songs 1:4a—

Song of Songs 1:15— *Your beautiful. You have beautiful eyes.*

Song of Songs 1:16a— *your delightful*

Song of Songs 4:9— *You have captivated my eyes*

Song of Songs 7:6— *your pleasant*

Jeremiah 31:3— *I'll love you forever. I am faithful to you.*

——Going the Distance Through Prayer——

Lover of Our Souls:

You left us the most encouraging and powerful note ever—Your inspired Word. How it has the capacity to lift us up and cause us to soar again. How it reminds us of Your unfailing love and continual presence. The gentle way You tell us You will never leave us or forsake us (Hebrews 13:5), how You have loved us with an everlasting love (Jeremiah 31:3), and how Your thoughts of us are precious and too numerous to count (Psalm 139:17-18). Please give us the words, the inspiration, and the discernment to know the perfect time to leave notes of encouragement to each other. Only You know when we will need to hear from each other with some healing, encouraging, life-giving words reminding us we are loved by one another and loved by You. Help us imitate Your example of love that speaks up and never fails.

— ❧ DAY 6 ❧ —

Giving Each Other Space

Very early in the morning, while it was still
dark, Jesus got up, left the house and went
off to a solitary place, where he prayed.

MARK 1:35

We live in an area of Southern California where it's extremely crowded. Traffic. Noise. Construction. Congestion. Cookie-cutter homes line suburban residential tracts everywhere the eye can see. Shopping centers, strip malls, and industrial complexes have sprung up on every speck of available land. It's enough to make you go crazy.

There are days (most every day, in fact) when I (Hugh) just need to leave the office and get away. To find a quiet place outdoors. To go hiking in the fresh air. To recharge my batteries while away from it all. That keeps me healthy, destressed, and better able to cope with the day-to-day demands of ministry. And once I've had that time, I can better process what comes my way the next day.

Marriage can get crowded at times, too. After all, you're two different people, with your own preferences and ways of doing things, living together in the same house. For what seems like forever. As John and Stasi Eldredge say in their book *Love and War,* "...bring together a man and a woman—two creatures who think, act, and feel so differently you would think they'd come from separate solar systems— and ask them to get along for the rest of their lives under the same roof. That is like taking Cinderella and Huck Finn, tossing them in a submarine and closing the hatch."[6] As I said, it's enough to make you go crazy at times.

So naturally, there are days when we just need our space. We need to get away, process our thoughts, experience the quiet, and hear from God.

For me, that involves getting away during the time when my day can become the most tense. Nothing does my soul better than to get into God's outdoors and experience Him there, away from the busyness and noise of the world even if it's only for an hour or two.

For Cindi, it means a drive to the park or a small lake near a housing development where she can get outside, breathe the air, talk to God, and get some perspective.

But maybe you don't have the luxury we do of getting away from it all—physically—to a nice place outdoors. Being self-employed in sunny Southern California may give us the edge on that. But you can still have your "space" by finding ways to recharge your—and your spouse's—soul.

Theresa's husband, John, has a demanding job, so she tries to give him the time to himself that he needs.

"His job is so stressful, I want to give him time to do the things he loves to do," she said. "He loves to play guitar and he likes to go to the beach and surf. Those are his two biggest loves besides his family, so I can express my love to him by giving him time for those things."

Alex and Mitzi are friends of ours whose lives overlap quite a bit. They own their own business, in which they work together out of their home. In addition, they minister alongside one another as the coleaders of a key ministry at our church. If that weren't enough, they are equally involved in their children's school and sports activities. As we said, their lives overlap quite a bit. And get this: They have one of the best marriages we've seen! So what gives?

Mitzi shared with me the secret to their success (and why they haven't yet destroyed each other).

"We work, live, and play together," Mitzi said. "That's a balancing act."

But they didn't always have the balance they have today. "When we first started our business it was difficult; we didn't know where to draw the boundaries. I was getting in his hair and he was getting in my hair, and it was disastrous."

So they had to define who does what. Alex is now the president of the company and Mitzi is the chief financial officer. He runs the business, solicits the work, and handles the conflict issues, while she pays the bills, balances the budget, and oversees the financial end of the business.

"The division of labor saved us," Mitzi said. Otherwise, their work arrangement was getting "crowded" and they found they were walking on top of each other.

Most couples, whether they work together or not, need their space. And it's possible one spouse will want or need more time with their spouse than the other. That's when it's helpful for both to have an agreement to give each other space.

Terri laughed as she recalled what happened after she told her husband she wanted him to spend more time with her. "All of a sudden he went everywhere I went, and he was right in my face every time I turned around. I finally had to say, 'Enough! I want you to spend more time with me, but not every waking moment!'" Terri and her husband laugh about it now, but he was just following her lead when she said, "I want you to spend more time with me."

Hugh needs more space than I do. And in the early years of our marriage I took it personally when he wanted to be by himself at times. I thought I was doing something that annoyed him, or I was, in some way, smothering him. But it wasn't just *me* he needed to have his space from—it was everyone. Being an introvert by nature, Hugh needed time alone to recharge.

In Scripture, we see there were times when the Son of God went away by Himself to a quiet place. On one occasion His disciples went out looking for Him, and when they found Him, they said, "Everyone's looking for You." Jesus made no apologies or excuses for slipping away by Himself. And instead of joining the crowd that was seeking

Him out, Jesus and His disciples went somewhere *else!* (Mark 1:35-37). Jesus needed to be alone, with His Father, praying, sitting in the silence. If the Son of God needed alone time, your husband or wife needs it, too.

Taking the Next Step

What are some ways you can give each other space? Absence *does* make the heart grow fonder—especially if the space your spouse needs is something you end up giving him or her as a gift.

For example, Hugh loves the musical group Celtic Woman. He could sit and listen to their music for hours. (And at times, he does.) I bought the two of us tickets to a concert one year, which we thoroughly enjoyed. A year later, partly due to the increased cost of the tickets and partly due to my schedule, I got him a ticket to attend the show by himself. He thoroughly enjoyed that as well. In fact, he still talks about the great evening he had just sitting alone and relishing in the music.

And a few years ago, when Hugh was experiencing personal burn-out from the ministry, we considered taking money out of savings for us to go to Israel for about 10 days. He needed to regenerate and we had talked all our lives of going to the Holy Land together. As I looked at the tour dates of the study group he preferred to travel with, I noticed that every date offered was already booked in my speaking schedule that spring. It was then that a friend said, "Let him go by himself. He needs this trip more than you do. Give him this time as a gift." Now I know many couples who wouldn't think of travelling so far away without each other. And I would never consider going there without him. But Hugh had travelled alone before. And he needed this trip more than he needed me to be able to come with him. In fact, deep in my heart I knew that he needed to go alone. So I asked him, "Hugh, what would you think about taking that trip by yourself?" His answer was thoughtful, but honest: "I would love for you to go with me, but I really need this trip. If you can't go, I would *love* to go alone." And he did. To this day, it's one of the gifts of space, rejuvenation, and growth that I feel I have given him and that he has most appreciated throughout our years together.

And when I've been on a book deadline, or just needing some time out of the house, Hugh has been equally generous with me, including sending me on trips back to my hometown to have some quiet time to write or encouraging me to stay an extra day or two when I go out of town to speak and have the opportunity to see family in the area.

What are some ways *you* can gift some space to your spouse?

It could be something simple like handing your husband or wife a $20 bill and saying "Why don't you enjoy a quiet meal to yourself. It's my gift to you." (If he or she is an introvert, they'll *love it.*)

It could be taking the kids for the day and telling your spouse, "This day is yours; do whatever you want. And I can't wait to hear, when the day is done, all that you did or didn't do…and how much you truly enjoyed it."

Or, it could be as simple as farming everyone out of the house for the evening so your spouse can have some alone time.

As much as you enjoy spending time together, recognize your spouse's need to have his or her space and relish in the quiet—without you—every now and then. You may find—as you give them some space—that they are more anxious to be with you once they've had it.

Cultivate a closer connection by lovingly giving each other space.

—— Going the Extra Mile ——

1. Talk with your spouse about the extent to which you both need your space. Are you giving each other too much or too little of what you both need? How can you find a healthy balance?

2. Talk about ways you can gift space to each other:

    a. What is a "space surprise" you'd like to receive sometime?

    b. In what situations or on what days do you find you need more space than usual?

3. Agree on a kind way to express to one another when you each need your space. (It's important that you be able to express this to each other without one of you taking it personally.)

——Going the Distance Through Prayer——

Lord, just as You often needed to slip away to a quiet place to get some rest, we need that, too. But help us to do it in a way that is healthy, that honors our spouse, and that is not hurtful in any way. You enjoy our togetherness, God, but You also want to get each of us alone to show us who we are in Your eyes, to speak to our hearts in ways we can't hear in the midst of our everyday routine, and to draw us closer to You in a way that You can do only when we are alone with You. Help us to recognize when the other needs space and to lovingly gift that to each other. Protect us while we are away from each other, and give us hearts that long to be back together again as we spend time apart. And may we long to have time with You so we can learn more of how to imitate Your love to each other.

— DAY 7 —

Extending Grace

Be completely humble and gentle; be patient,
bearing with one another in love.

EPHESIANS 4:2

Rich and Ashley spent an entire weekend doing yard work together. First they pulled out a tree in their front yard; then they tilled the soil so they could replant grass in some areas where it had never been able to grow. As they churned the ground with a rototiller they hit some buried rocks, which bumped and clanged against the blades and sent the machine out of control. But once those rocks were out, the soil became much easier to prepare for planting. They shared with us, too, how very sore they were from weeding, pulling out rocks, and trying to control a rototiller that would go crazy every time it unearthed a hard object. We laughed together and pondered how all they had gone through sounded a lot like life, and in particular, marriage.

The next day, I (Cindi) thought a lot about that conversation. And I asked God to take a rototiller to my life and turn up the rocks that are hidden in the soil of my heart. I asked Him to take out any hardness or problem that is preventing me from yielding fruit in my life. I found myself asking God to smooth out the soil so more fruit could be planted and grown in me.

As the saying goes, when you try to do something right, that's usually when you mess up! Wouldn't you agree? Sure enough, that evening after dinner, the rocks started being churned up in the soil of my heart and I was verbally critical toward my husband.

The next morning, I sent Hugh an e-mail:

> I knew God wanted to do a work in me when it came to writing this book on how couples can walk together. I just didn't know there was so much He had to unearth in me in order to replant. Taking Rich's illustration on Sunday of rototilling the ground and unearthing some rocks, there are quite a few rocks hidden in the soil of my heart and they surface now and then as unresolved wounds and bitterness, and I am so sorry for that. I truly want to be Christlike in every way, and that means denying myself and what I feel I have a right to, and it appears that my marriage is one way that I am still NOT Christlike. There's still too much of me.
>
> Please know that I don't want to cause you pain. I really do need you to love me as Christ does because I realize there may not be anything left in me at this point that is still loveable.
>
> Humbly, Cindi

Hugh's reply was one that extended grace.

> Of course I will always try to love you as Christ does. We both have rocks under the soil and dysfunctions that God is still redeeming. I appreciate you sharing these words from your heart and there is still much to love about Cindi.

The Bible says it is by grace (undeserved favor) that we are saved and not by anything that we do—it is the gift of God, so that we can't boast in our salvation (Ephesians 2:8-9).

Hugh and I have come to believe that it is by grace (undeserved favor) that we are loved by each other, too, not because of anything we do. It is a gift from each other so that we can't boast in ourselves about how good of a spouse we are.

When I (Cindi) am aware of how unlovable I can be at times, it makes me more loving to my husband, who, by the grace of God, still puts up with me. Now compare that with the attitude that comes so quickly and naturally to our minds: *I deserve better than that. He has no right to treat me that way. I can do better somewhere else.* And so on.

A person who extends grace says, "I'd be honored if you would still love me." It's humbling. But it's how we are loved by God and how we must learn to love each other.

Our friends, Alex and Mitzi, shared with us how they are able to extend grace toward one another. They have learned to model God's love toward each other. And they have taken seriously His command for them to love God first, and then love others.

They have adopted Matthew 22:37-39 as their life verse for their marriage, family, and business: "'Love the Lord your God with all your heart and with all your soul and with all your mind.' This is the first and greatest commandment. And the second is like it: 'Love your neighbor as yourself.'"

"Follow those two commandments—keep them in front of you at all times and everything works out," Mitzi told me over breakfast one morning. "And that means love your husband even when he's being a jerk. And love your wife even when she's being a brat. Love even when you don't feel like it."

Extend grace, even when it's not deserved.

For Alex and Mitzi, extending grace comes down to forgiving each other quickly. And that happens by talking about issues immediately and then getting over them and moving on. Nothing's allowed to stew.

"We are both stubborn, strong-willed people," Mitzi told me. "If something hurts our feelings, we're right on it right away and we get it settled. I will say, 'That really hurt me,' and he will respond with, 'Whoa, wait a minute. I didn't mean it that way.' Quick forgiveness humbles you. It leaves no room for pride and selfishness, which are the two biggest destroyers of a marriage."

Our friends, Dan and Chris, have learned in their 21 years of marriage to choose carefully what they make a big deal of.

"We have to choose our battles," Dan said. "I have to try not to make a big deal every time something bothers me. If something still bothers me the next day, then I'll bring it up."

His wife, Chris, said that as a woman sometimes that's a little more difficult to do.

"Women are often passionate about what they want in their marriage, how they want their lives to be, how they feel about the way their husband is responding, so petty things sometimes seem like a big deal." But she's also found that for her, dealing with a situation right away helps it not become a big deal.

Sometimes to extend grace means resolving quietly to not react to a situation or comment that annoyed you so that the other person never even realizes it bothered you. That's difficult at times. But that is unconditional love in action. That is extending grace.

Taking the Next Step

So how do you become a person who quickly extends grace?

Be humble and remember you are human, too. Because you, like your spouse, are not perfect, that means you too make careless mistakes, just like the mistake your spouse made that is really grating on your nerves. Maybe your spouse's tardiness has become a real problem. Realize that you have also been late before.

Don't assign motives. That often means taking yourself out of the equation. Chris said that her husband doesn't remember things like he used to. "That's a struggle for me because sometimes I confuse that with him not listening and paying attention to me, when that might not actually be the case." Grace says, "I won't make this about me or how you're treating me." It says, "I won't try to figure out why you said or did that. I will just consider you didn't mean it the way it came across." Using the example of your tardy spouse, realize there may be a good reason he or she is late, and it's not solely because he or she just doesn't respect your time.

Be understanding. The easiest way to remember to extend grace is to realize you are capable of doing the very same things (or similar things) your spouse has done that you dislike. For every five things that Hugh does that irritate me, I'm sure there are at least *ten* things that I do that irritate him! By being understanding and extending grace, you are hopefully putting on reserve a deposit in your spouse's bank of understanding so when you are someday in the same situation, he or she will extend grace to you as well.

——Going the Extra Mile——

1. Tell your spouse the one area in which you feel you need the most grace. Then ask about the one area in your mate's life in which he or she needs grace as well.

2. What do the following verses say about extending grace to your spouse?

   Proverbs 15:1— *a use kind words in response*

   Ephesians 4:2— *be gentle and show love with humility.*

   Colossians 3:12-14— *love and forgive using christ's example*

   James 1:19— *listen first then speak and controlling your wrath*

——Going the Distance Through Prayer——

God, it is by Your grace that You choose to love us in spite of all of our weaknesses, failures, and mistakes. It is by Your grace that You continue to love us even when we are unlovable in Your sight. Teach us to extend that kind of grace and love toward each other. On days when we feel irritated with each other, remind us of Your unconditional love and that You never give up on us. On days when we are impatient toward each other, remind us of Your longsuffering toward us. And help us to extend that kind of unconditional love and patience so that we never give up on each other. Remove us from the element, God, when we begin to take each other's actions personally and help us to be kind and tenderhearted, forgiving one another as You have forgiven us. May we be a couple who stands out to others as two people who truly extend grace toward one another. May we each learn better to bear all things, believe all things, hope all things, and endure all things for Your pleasure, Lord, and for our unity with each other.

— ☙ DAY 8 ❧ —
Taking a Walk

As you therefore have received Christ
Jesus the Lord, so walk in Him

COLOSSIANS 2:6 NASB

There is something therapeutic about taking a walk.

We live in a society that is racing at such a rapid pace these days. We are literally on the *run*. Oh, to slow down, take a walk, and enjoy life—together.

My Uncle Owen and Aunt Alice have discovered the beauty of taking a walk together. Married 53 years, they have raised four children and weathered much of life together. And now, three times a week, they enjoy the simple pleasure of walking together.

"We don't run," Alice said with a laugh, reminding me (Cindi) that they are both in their mid 70s now. "We just walk. We walk and think a little as we walk."

"Talking isn't so important," Owen added. "When you're walking, you can be together and you don't have to talk. And other times it's good to have that time together because we do get more of a chance to talk."

Alice said, "Sometimes one of us says something and it puts us together on a thought process and the other one of us doesn't need to respond right away."

"People need to learn how to process that way and use that," Owen said.

"And if you don't want to say anything right away, you can just say, 'Let me catch my breath,'" Alice added.

While they thoroughly enjoy their regular routine of walking together, it wasn't always possible for them to do that. For most of their married life, they were raising children. They don't remember taking time to walk back then.

"When our kids were little it was harder for us to get away from them to talk about how I corrected one of them, and stuff like that," Owen recalled. "Communication is more difficult when the kids are small." How he wishes now that he and Alice had taken the time to get away together on a short walk, to reconnect with each other, to communicate outside the presence of the children, and just be together.

Alice said that would've been nice. "Owen was with the boys at sports activities a lot of times and I would stay at home with our youngest. We weren't together as much back then. Now we're in the season of life where we can spend time together."

To hear Alice and Owen talk about what they wish they'd done together years ago, and seeing how much they enjoy doing that now, makes us want to take more walks with each other—today.

My cousin, Tami (now married with four children of her own), marvels at the close relationship her parents have today.

"Growing up, I didn't notice it as much," she said, reflecting on her parents' sense of togetherness. "One time on a family vacation, we were walking through a touristy town and my dad was holding my mom's hand. My brother and I looked at each other and laughed because it wasn't typical for them to do that. Because they were so wrapped up in their family and what the kids needed, and they were also very involved in church, we never saw them as particularly close. But now—in their retirement years—they are."

Listen closely…can you hear it? It's the wisdom that rings through the words of a couple who has been together more than 50 years. We drew three lessons from what we heard about Owen and Alice and the closeness they share today:

1. Don't miss the opportunity to walk together today. (You don't want your children or others saying you were too

busy to spend time with each other as they were growing up.)

2. If you feel like you and your spouse are two ships that pass in the night, the day will come (as happened with Owen and Alice) when your schedules will slow down and you will have much more time to spend with each other.

3. Invest in your relationship *today* by doing what otherwise might not happen until tomorrow—or in your 70s.

Now that Owen and Alice are nearing 80 years old, their days have slowed down considerably. No daily jobs to report to. No kids' activities to rush off to. No tyranny of the urgent with home, school, work, homework, sports, and church activities. But it isn't just their schedules that have slowed. They too have slowed down. They now walk, not run, through life. Perhaps it is because of the wisdom they've gained through the years to slow down and take time to "seize the day." Perhaps it's the slower pace of life that comes with age and declining health. Or maybe it's just the ever-present awareness that the time they have left with each other is more precious than ever as it draws nearer to a close. And so they walk while they still have the opportunity. While they still can. While they still have each other.

As Tami and I talked about the closeness her parents share, and how they are growing older together, Tami choked up. She said, "I can't imagine either one of them without the other."

They are the epitome of togetherness. They are truly life partners. They walk together. Literally.

Taking the Next Step

Do you and your spouse take the opportunity to walk together? Maybe you don't have the luxury of that because your schedules are so hectic. But when you are both deliberate and intentional about spending time together, you can make it happen.

To say, "I don't have time" is a lie. We make time to do whatever is most important to us. We make time for the investments that are the most worthwhile to us.

Hugh and I often walk, but by ourselves. While Hugh is working and when I need a breather from writing or deadline pressures or laundry, I go for a walk to clear my mind, get a little exercise, and enjoy the great outdoors. (Remember that chapter on giving each other space?) And Hugh goes for walks later in the day so he can experience the outdoors as well as challenge his body through extended hikes and climbs. Hugh has some favorite hills he enjoys hiking through to stay in shape. But every once in a while he sets the "calorie burn" incentive aside and goes at a bit of a slower pace and has me join him. We both enjoy our individual walking routines, but the times we walk *together* are precious.

There is something about walking together that builds intimacy.

In the Bible, we're told about a man named Enoch. He did a lot of walking. In fact, Scripture says, "Enoch walked with God 300 years… then he was no more, because God took him away."[7] Wow…what intimacy must have developed between that old man and God during those 300 years of walking together!

It's interesting that the passage doesn't say Enoch *ran* with God. Or Enoch *knew* God for 300 years. Or even that Enoch *followed* God. Rather, he *walked* with Him. I wonder if, at times, Enoch just disappeared on one of those long walks with God in the late afternoon and didn't come back till much after dinner time. Then when God finally took him, I wonder if at first everyone thought Enoch was coming home late because of another late-evening walk with God. Only he never ended up coming back.

The point is that during those long walks together, the friendship and intimacy between God and Enoch grew.

After Jesus ascended from the grave He walked this earth for another 40 days, appearing to more than 500 people during that time. Two of the people He appeared to were walking on a road toward a village called Emmaus, discussing the events of Jesus' death and resurrection. Jesus, who at first went unrecognized by them, walked along the road with them. He asked about what they were discussing, and then explained all that was said about Him in the Scriptures from the writings of Moses through the writings of the prophets. Imagine that! Jesus Himself was unfolding the truths and wisdom of the Scriptures and explaining how they pertained to Himself. And the men didn't even know they were talking with Jesus until just before He disappeared from their midst.[8]

Do you ever wonder what those two men would have missed had they been speed walking (to burn extra calories) and had no time to slow down and chat? What if they had just whipped right by Jesus? Or what if they had been too wrapped up in their own thoughts as they walked (as I, Cindi, tend to do) to take the time to listen and engage in conversation with Him? Or what if they already had places to go and people to see such that they missed the walk altogether and the most important one they could have met—God in human flesh, unfolding words of wisdom?

Now, that's probably not going happen on one of *your* walks. (That is, God appearing in human flesh and physically walking with you.) But you have a partner, in the flesh, with whom you can walk. What wonderful things you can discover as you take the time to walk with your spouse. But you won't be able to walk with him or her on this earth forever. Eventually, failed health may slow one of you down to where you can't walk together anymore. Eventually, you or your spouse may need a cane or a wheelchair or a replaced knee or have some other debilitating condition and you may find it difficult to get out and walk at all. One day, one of you will leave this earth, leaving the other to walk alone.

Take the advice of Uncle Owen and Aunt Alice. Walk together *now*—while you have the chance. Don't wait until you are in your seventies and wish you'd walked more when you were younger. There's no better time than today to start walking together—literally.

—— Going the Extra Mile ——

At what times or occasions can you two walk together? If you are deliberate and intentional about it, taking time to walk together just might become a reality. Think through the following options and decide which would work best for the two of you:

- Sunday afternoons, even if you have to bring the kids along for a while. This can be a hand-holding, together time for the two of you.

- Once or twice a week, after dinner when the air is cool, providing you with the opportunity to catch up with each other and reflect on the day. (Start with only one day a week if you can. One day is far better than none!)

- Saturday mornings—as an early start to your day—and then reward yourself with breakfast together.

- Holidays—walk together in the morning before the plans set in and family arrives and the meal preparation starts.

- Every first or last or fifth Saturday (or Sunday) of the month. Plan ahead for it, write it on the calendar, and look forward to it. These regularly scheduled walks will help you make a memory or establish a tradition together.

——Going the Distance Through Prayer——

Lord, slow us down so we can enjoy one of the simple pleasures in life—walking together. We long to know the intimacy with You and each other that Enoch knew when he walked with You those 300 years. Please place the desire in our hearts to walk closer together in this way, help us arrange it in our schedules, and then give us the discipline to keep that appointment with each other. We invite You to walk along with us so we can thoroughly enjoy Your presence and each other's. Your Word says "a cord of three strands is not quickly broken" (Ecclesiastes 4:12). Be that third strand in our relationship and bind us together as we take the time to walk together. May we (and our children, as well) look back on our lives and remember that we took the time for each other by taking the time to walk—together.

Checking the Baggage

Jesus said, "Come to me, all of you who are weary
and carry heavy burdens, and I will give you rest."

MATTHEW 11:28 NLT

When the airlines started charging fees for checked luggage, I (Cindi) started taking a lot more with me in my carry-on bag. And you know what? Doing that made my trip a lot more difficult (and more miserable). My shoulders and back became terribly sore from lugging a heavy and overstuffed carry-on bag, and by the time I arrived at my destination, I was exhausted.

Often we approach marriage the same way. We take way too much baggage into it. And we prefer to cling to a lot of it when our lives, relationships, and homes would be much happier if we would just check in everything at the gate and let it go.

God is the perfect baggage-check attendant at the airport, if you want to think about it that way. He asks if He can carry your load for you. He knows this journey called marriage will become quite uncomfortable if you choose to take certain baggage along. He wants you to make this journey without the burdens that could weigh you down.

In Matthew 11:28-30, Jesus said, "Come to me, all you who are weary and burdened [with too much stuff] and I will give you rest [relief]. Take my yoke upon you and learn from me, for I am gentle and humble in heart…For my yoke is easy and my burden is light."

God knows what's around the bend. And He wants us to approach life together without all the extra baggage that can weigh us down. So He tells us, "Take my yoke upon you and learn from me…For my yoke is easy and my burden is light."

In another translation, Jesus' words read like this: "I won't lay anything heavy or ill-fitting on you. Keep company with me and you'll learn to live freely and lightly."[9]

If we're going to not only survive this journey called marriage, but draw closer to one another, we're going to need to live freely and lightly…without the stuff that weighs us down.

What is God's load that He asks us to take upon ourselves? What is the heaviest thing He asks us to carry? We can answer that question by looking at what Jesus considered our greatest requirement. When a religious leader asked Jesus what is the greatest commandment, Jesus said:

> "'Love the Lord your God with all your heart and with all your soul and with all your mind.' This is the first and greatest commandment. And the second is like it: 'Love your neighbor as yourself'" (Matthew 22:37-39).

Imagine that. God's burden on us is to love Him with all our hearts and to love our neighbor (including our spouse) as ourselves. That is not a burden—it is a privilege! That "load" He will share with us is easy and light, for He will enable us to love Him and our spouse as we have been loved.

Think about it. The only load we are expected to carry through life is the burden to love God and others as much as we love ourselves. And that load, Jesus tells us, is easy and light. It frees us. It brings us joy.

If you're like most couples, you have not completely let go of the excess baggage in order to carry the one load you are asked to carry. There are probably some things you're still holding onto over and above the "love God and your neighbor" carry-on. Those things need to be checked at the gate so you can let go of them.

Taking the Next Step

If we were to do an inventory of the most common baggage that couples carry with them, the list would look like this:

- *Victimization baggage*—This carry-on item says, "Because of what happened to me, I will always be or feel this way."

- *Insecurity baggage*—This one says, "Because of what I believe about myself, there's nothing you can say that will convince me otherwise."

- *Past baggage*—This carry-on says, "Because of how I was raised, this is how I will always be."

- *Relational baggage*—This leads us to say, "I was hurt in the past; that is why I will never really trust you."

- *Personal baggage*—"This is what I struggle with, and I will never let you in."

- *Excess baggage*—"I am carrying so many different bags and wounds that I don't even know which is which anymore."

Now, do any of those bags hold good, positive things for your journey with one another? No. They each represent dead weight. They will drag you down. They will burden you. They will cause you pain. And they will keep you from enjoying the journey.

Give your loved one a gift today and drop the bags that are weighing down your life and your future together.

Second Corinthians 5:17 (and the first part of verse 18) says, "Anyone who belongs to Christ is a new person. The past is forgotten, and everything is new...God has done it all!" (CEV). That means the bags from your past that you feel obliged to carry contain nothing about who you are *today* as a child of God. Won't you let Him take that load off your shoulders so you can love your spouse more openly and freely?

Go ahead. You can do it. Hand that baggage over to the Only One who can take it and give you peace, rest, and joy in return.

Experience a closer connection today by checking the baggage at the gate.

——Going the Extra Mile——

We certainly don't want to minimize the difficulty that may be involved in surrendering baggage to God that has been with you for maybe as long as you can remember. So, prayerfully, go through these steps. You may also want to check out additional resources on this subject. We highly recommend Neil Anderson's *Freedom in Christ* resources.[10]

1. Talk with your spouse about what you have carried into marriage but haven't meant to.

2. Read the following verses (you may even want to commit a couple to memory to help you leave those bags behind you). Commit these areas to the Lord in prayer and write today's date next to these verses in your Bible as a reminder of your commitment to let go of the baggage.

   2 Corinthians 5:17 (The old is gone; the new has come.)

   Galatians 2:20 (I—and my issues—have been crucified with Christ.)

   Matthew 11:28-30 (Take God's load upon you, not your own.)

   Philippians 3:13-14 (Forget what lies behind and look forward to what's ahead.)

——Going the Distance Through Prayer——

Take some time to pray this prayer of release with your partner. As you do, gain confidence from 1 John 5:14-15, which tells us, "If we ask anything according to his will, he hears us. And if we know that he hears us—whatever we ask—we know that we have what we asked of him."

> Lord, we want to honor You in our marriage by giving to You everything that You never meant for us to carry on our journey together. We give to You our past hurts, our insecurities, our past failures, and our pain. We give to You unresolved wounds in past relationships as well as unresolved wounds between the two of us. We place at Your feet our expectations that we've carried with us since the day we married. We give to You our suitcase of dashed hopes and stored-up bitterness. Take it all, Lord Jesus, and give us Your peace in return. Let us experience the relief that comes from handing our burdens to You and knowing we never have to carry them again.
>
> Lord, show us each day the joy that comes from faithfully carrying the only load You have asked us to carry—Your command to love You with all our heart, soul, mind, and strength, and to love each other as we love ourselves. God, only You can give us a love for each other that equals and even surpasses the love we have for ourselves.
>
> Lord, we truly want to walk together lightly and freely. Lead the way before us. And don't let us ever look back to pick up what we've left behind.
>
> In the name of Jesus—who carries our burdens, lightens our load, lifts our heads, and makes all things new—Amen.

—— ❧ DAY 10 ❧ ——

Finding Encouraging Words

Do not let any unwholesome talk come out of your mouths,
but only what is helpful for building others up according
to their needs, that it may benefit those who listen.

EPHESIANS 4:29

Debbie was discouraged and wondered where God was. A close friend of hers and Dan's had just been killed in an accident overseas, leaving behind a beautiful wife and four young children. Debbie was questioning how God could have allowed this to happen.

It was then that Dan came to the rescue with encouraging words for his wife.

"Remember, Deb, God loves those children and knows just what they need. Don't focus on the tragedy. Instead, look at how the Lord sovereignly and graciously prepared the family to endure this loss."

Dan explained to her that, as a military family, years of moving and deployments overseas had taught the wife and children how to endure change and function without Dad.

"Just before Jim was called to his heavenly home, God gave the family a long period of rest and relaxation, an opportunity to make lasting memories together. As the family goes into an uncertain future, God will keep them in His hands the same way He has always held them."

Dan's well-thought-out, compassionate words made all the difference in the world to Debbie, who, for a brief moment, was questioning the very nature and character of God.

If the health of your relationship could be determined solely by the words exchanged between the two of you, how healthy would your relationship be?

Back on Day 4, we talked about "Praising the Positive" by "filling your minds and meditating on things true, noble, reputable, authentic, compelling, gracious—the best, not the worst; the beautiful, not the ugly; things to praise, not things to curse" (Philippians 4:8 MSG). If we were to apply Philippians 4:8 not only to what we *think* about one another, but to what we *say* to each other, we'd be well on our way toward a closer connection.

Consider the impact of it. If you insert the words "speech" and "speaking" in that verse you get this: "Keep your [speech] on whatever is true, pure, right, holy, friendly, and proper. Don't ever stop [speaking] about what is truly worthwhile and worthy of praise" (Philippians 4:8 CEV). Puts a whole new spin on it, doesn't it? In other words, think before you speak to one another. And then speak well!

Ephesians 4:29 tells us, "Do not let any unwholesome talk come out of your mouths, but only what is helpful for building others up according to their needs, that it may benefit those who listen."

Let's look at that verse in a few other translations:

- "Let everything you say be good and helpful, so that your words will be an encouragement to those who hear them" (NLT).

- "Stop all your dirty talk. Say the right thing at the right time and help others by what you say" (CEV).

- "Watch the way you talk. Let nothing foul or dirty come out of your mouth. Say only what helps, each word a gift" (MSG).

Each word a *gift*—have you ever thought about your speech in that way? We can wound each other greatly with our words. Or we can give to each other greatly with the words we say to one another.

We asked several men to tell us the kinds of words they would consider gifts when coming from their wives. This was what their "gift list" included:

- I'm proud of you.
- I admire you.
- I respect you for _____.
- I believe in you.
- You made me so proud when you _____.
- You can do it.

In other words, ladies, your husband wants to feel respected, admired, and capable. He needs to know you believe in his ability to provide for you, to be a good father, to handle money effectively, to overcome challenges in his personal as well as his married life. He also needs to know you still desire him physically. So give him the gift of encouragement by affirming him in those ways—often.

We also asked some women to tell us the kind of words they would consider gifts when coming from their husbands. And their "gift list" looked like this:

- I love you. (Even if you prefer to show it instead, we still need to hear it.)
- You are beautiful.
- You mean the world to me.
- I appreciate you.
- I respect what you do.
- You do that well.
- You are very capable at _____.

In other words (or in *these* words), wives want to feel desired, cherished, and appreciated. Women also want to feel needed by their husbands. They were created to be helpers (Genesis 2:18), and they need to know when they're actually helping. They also need your expressions of tenderness, which help affirm to them that you hold them in high regard.

Taking the Next Step

We've talked about the value of encouraging words. And most important of all is that you know what *your* spouse needs to hear from *you*. Debbie was struggling to make sense of a situation. When Dan spoke to her, he didn't rebuke her for feeling the way she did, nor did he try to convince her to feel differently. Rather, he spoke compassionately from his heart in a way that her heart would understand. He helped her see something he saw and knew she needed to see as well.

What words or phrases, said in all honesty, resonate as a gift to your spouse? That is a question you need to ask each other. And you need to remember each other's answers...so you will have the right words when they're needed.

Find encouraging words for one another and use them often. That is another way of walking together and cultivating a closer connection.

—— Going the Extra Mile ——

1. Take some time to write down—in the space below—the phrases you each would like to hear from each other.

   Encouraging words *HE* would like to receive:

   Encouraging words *SHE* would like to receive:

2. Write down Ephesians 4:29 on an index card and put it where you will see it often to remind you to only say what is encouraging and uplifting to your spouse. Better yet, commit that verse to memory. It's an investment well worth the effort.

(What you fill your mind and heart with will eventually flow out of your mouth.)

3. What do the following verses say about how we should speak to each other?

Psalm 19:14— *Let my words & thoughts be pleasing to God*

Proverbs 12:18— *Harsh words hurt. Wise words bring healing.*

Proverbs 15:1— *Harsh words bring anger. Soft words stop anger.*

Colossians 3:16-17— *Do everything in God's name & in thankfulness to him.*

Colossians 4:6— *Use your words graciously to bring out the best in others*

——Going the Distance Through Prayer——

Lord, You are the Living Word. During Your sojourn on earth, when You spoke, Your words brought life. Your words raised people from the dead, enabled the blind to see, healed the sick, and strengthened lame legs to walk. May our words, as well, bring life to each other. May we build each other up with our words rather than tear each other down. May we heal hurts in each other's lives through the tender salve of our words. May we not say a thing if it isn't true, noble, right, pure, lovely, admirable, excellent, or praiseworthy.

God, give us insight into what we need to say to bind each

other's wounds after a rough day, to lighten each other's loads in the midst of tension, and to inspire and instill courage in the other. May we as a couple speak wisely toward one another and everyone else we come in contact with. Show us, Lord Jesus, how to give the gift of encouraging words to each other every day of our lives.

May the words of our mouths and the meditations of our hearts—toward each other—be pleasing in Your sight, O God.

— DAY 11 —

Making a Memory

Relish life with the spouse you love
each and every day of your precarious life.
Each day is God's gift. It's all you get in exchange
for the hard work of staying alive.
Make the most of each one!

ECCLESIASTES 9:9 MSG

I was really upset with Hugh. I can't remember what he did or didn't
do, but I remember thinking that I'd just about had it with him! So,
on much of an impulse, I picked up the phone and booked a marriage
conference.

As I dialed, the thought occurred to me: *We've been married almost
20 years and have never even attended a marriage conference.* That made
me even madder. *Well, he's gonna go to one, then.* I discovered that pastors go free of charge, so why not? I also discovered the next conference
in the western states was in Las Vegas. And I had never been there. *Fine,
we're going to Vegas.* I booked us some cheap flights, a modest room at
the expensive hotel where the conference was being held, and even some
tickets to the *Star Trek Experience,* a limited-time attraction that would
give Hugh, a bona fide Trekker since childhood, something to look forward to the day before the conference. And then I called Hugh at work.

"Hello," he answered in the cautious tone he maintains when he sus-
pects his wife might be ready to go ballistic on him.

"We're going to Vegas," I told him.

Silence on the other end of the phone.

"I was so mad at you, I booked us a marriage conference," I explained. "And we're going to the one in Vegas. I also got us tickets to the *Star Trek Experience.*"

"Cool," was Hugh's response, with somewhat of a lift in his voice. And it turned out to be the best spontaneous decision I've ever made in the wake of being really upset with Hugh.

Upon arriving at the hotel where the conference was being held, we were pleasantly surprised to find that we'd been given a complimentary upgrade to the honeymoon suite. Was it because Hugh was a pastor and we were attending for the first time? Was it a fluke on the part of the hotel when they set aside the rooms? Or was it one of those unexplainable "God things" because we were finally investing in our marriage in a tangible way? To this day, we don't know. But the room was gorgeous and far more expensive than we would've ever been able to afford.

Besides the luxuriously romantic room, we soon discovered that getting away from it all and intentionally investing in our marriage made for a wonderful weekend together. We still talk of that trip to Las Vegas together as one of the best trips we've ever taken.

Our first Weekend to Remember marriage conference[11] became one of our favorite memories together as well. Out of a miserable situation (at least I was feeling miserable at the time I booked the conference) came a very special memory. (And on second thought, our second and third Weekend to Remember conferences—which were local, only about a half hour from our home—were just as enjoyable and memorable.)

What makes for a good memory between the two of you?

Bob recalled a special memory with his wife, Mary Beth, which occurred not too long ago. They were backpacking about six miles into Yosemite, where their daughter worked. "It wasn't just six miles; it was a *torturous* straight-up climb," Bob recalled.

Torturous? Yet it's a good memory? "It was something we were doing together and she was having a hard time and yet our daughter, Aili, was in a dress and flip-flops! It was a challenge that we got through together." The altitude, plus a bad hip for Mary Beth, plus a straight-up hike of 1500 feet meant they hiked 30-50 feet at a time and then stopped to catch their breath. "Mary Beth hung in there and she did it," Bob said. "I was very proud of her."

For Mary Beth, the hike is *not* one of her favorite memories. But she was touched that Bob considered it a together moment in which they rose above a challenge. In fact, her husband teaching her how to handle the great outdoors *is* one of her favorite memories.

"My father was not a big vacation person and we *never* camped, so right after we married, Bob taught me how to camp, and that's a favorite memory." She laughed when she considered the torturous climb into Yosemite and how she didn't do too well. "Thirty-five years later, Bob is *still* teaching me how to camp," she said.

Lance and Pam recall a special memory that wasn't about pleasant circumstances either. "We went a week without knowing whether our son, Scott, had junior rheumatoid arthritis or leukemia because both show the same symptoms. We truly gave our son up to the Lord during that time," Pam said. "The Lord whispered to our hearts, 'I gave My Son for you; are you willing to give up your son to Me?' It was a very sweet, emotional time for us as parents."

Lance and Pam also took a cross-country road trip in their fifth wheel about five years ago. Lance had recently had a potentially cancerous spot removed from his chin and the doctor had told them to relax for a couple of weeks. "So we took off in our trailer," Pam said. "We went to Yosemite, going through Nevada, Idaho, and Montana, then we went all the way to Nebraska. We came home through Colorado, Utah, and Nevada. We stayed in a trailer park each night. One night in Colorado we stayed in a Wal-mart parking lot because we couldn't find a park…and that trip is *still* a great memory of time spent together!"

When I (Cindi) turned 30, Hugh surprised me with a one-night stay at a hotel. It was fairly local and the hotel was nothing extraordinary, but the room he booked—called the president's suite—was out of this world! It had a fireplace and an in-room Jacuzzi, and there was even an ice cream place within walking distance. The thought Hugh put into booking that place and surprising me with it made for a wonderful memory.

Our friends Dan and Chris recalled a special memory for us: "We went up to Sonoma once, rented a convertible Mustang, and went driving through the countryside listening to music." They did something out of the ordinary, and it became a memory.

Now that doesn't mean we must book a hotel together or go out and travel with one another or spend lots of money to make special memories. Simple things can make for wonderful memories too.

Our friends Don and Barbara have made special memories out of a yearly tradition. "We reread our wedding vows to each other on our anniversary," Barbara told me. "It's nothing formal—we can do it in a hotel room, on a beach, at a restaurant, or at home. It's one of those things we do to be deliberate and intentional."

Taking the Next Step

What can the two of you do—today—to create a memory with each other? Maybe you can try doing one of the application exercises in this book that you haven't yet tried doing. Or, maybe you can do something your spouse has always wanted to do but you haven't done it yet because you're not sure you can afford it, or whether you have the time to do it, or you've been hesitant because there are risks involved.

In his book *Say Goodbye to Regret*, author Robert Jeffress encourages couples to build memories with each other. He says he sees many couples fruitlessly marking time in their marriages by waiting for the kids to grow up and move out, waiting until the mortgage is paid, and waiting to retire.

> That husband or wife is God's gift to you to enjoy *now*. Do you have a hobby you both would enjoy? Why not start it today? Do you have a trip you've dreamed of taking together? Borrow the money if you have to and go. There's no guarantee that there will be a tomorrow. As a pastor I deal with many people who have lost their mate. Without a doubt, those who are able to cope best are those who have a storehouse of memories with their mate from which to draw.[12]

That makes us think of Bill and June. Their granddaughter, Brooke, came up with the idea to throw them a big party for their forty-ninth wedding anniversary because they were both longtime San Francisco 49ers fans. So Bill and June's children and grandchildren got together and threw them a huge 49ers-theme wedding anniversary party. Bill wore his favorite 49ers shirt. The cake was decorated to look like a 49ers football helmet. All the stops were pulled out as if it were their golden anniversary.

"Who has a big celebration on their forty-ninth?" June said to me, marveling how she and the children and grandchildren had no idea that her beloved Bill wouldn't be with them by the time their fiftieth wedding anniversary rolled around. Shortly before their forty-ninth wedding anniversary, Bill was diagnosed with bone cancer (which the children and grandchildren didn't know about as they planned and attended the party). Five short months later, he passed away. That forty-ninth anniversary party became one of Bill and June's most precious memories.

So what have the two of you longed to do together? What is one thing you'd like to see or one place you'd like to go or one thing you'd like to experience together before one of you leaves this earth? Make that memory today. There's no guarantee that there will be a tomorrow.

——Going the Extra Mile——

1. What are a few of your favorite memories together? List them here, along with a one-word summary that describes each one:

2. Now what are some memories that you would like to make together? Dream a little and record your thoughts here:

3. What does Ecclesiastes 9:7-10 say about how you should approach life, and how does that apply to making a memory while you can? Rewrite the passage here in your own words:

——Going the Distance Through Prayer——

Lord, throughout Your Word You stressed the importance of Your chosen people remembering what You had done for them. They were to remember how You brought them out of bondage in Egypt and led them through the Red Sea on dry land. They were to remember how You parted the waters of the Jordan River so they could walk through it. They were to remember the manna that You dropped from heaven so they would be filled.

Lord, help us to remember the many times You have rained down blessings on us. May we never forget the precious times we've experienced together and the blessings You've sent our way that have amounted to special memories between the two of us. And, Lord, please give us both creativity and a sense of urgency to make a memory every chance we have, knowing we are not guaranteed a tomorrow. Teach us to number our days so that we may gain a heart of wisdom. And, as the psalmist said, "Oh! Teach us to live well! Teach us to live wisely and well!"[13]

—— ❧ DAY 12 ❧ ——

Sharing Your Heart

Someone's thoughts may be as deep as the ocean,
but if you are smart, you will discover them.

PROVERBS 20:5 CEV

I will never forget that evening. It was one of those times when something within me was longing for a closer connection with my husband. I can't really explain it. All I know is that he must have known it. Or maybe he didn't. But when we sat together at a favorite restaurant and he looked at me from across the table and said, "Tonight, I want to share with you some thoughts and feelings that I've been writing down through the years" and opened up his journal in front of me, something in my heart skipped a beat and changed toward him. I felt there was a room inside of his soul that he had unlocked and let me into. And it was wonderful.

Hugh read to me portions of poetry that he had written as a young man in his early twenties. A line from a song that touched his heart at one point in his life. A saying that described what he was feeling during a certain season of his life. A memory that touched his heart that I didn't know about. An expressed wish or dream he'd been pondering in his heart. Page after page of the inside of my man's heart. It opened a wider door for me through which I could see who he really was. If ever there was a time in which I could have stopped the clock and just basked in the extension of a moment, that would have been it.

Okay, men—Hugh here. Just a few words for those of you who

have been hesitant or dismissive about keeping a logbook of your thoughts. For me, there's a difference between a diary and a journal, and I'm definitely the kind of guy who journals. I don't know about you, but when I think of the word *diary,* a picture comes to mind of a pigtailed teen writing secret, intimate thoughts into a little book with flowers and ponies on the cover and a lock on the binding—which she keeps hidden in her hope chest.

Thankfully, that's not the only option for us when it comes to writing down a motivational quote, that flash of artistic genius, or a string of words that somehow describes a memorable moment in time. What I have discovered is that God has things to say to us or to show us that are so profound that I don't want to forget them. And more often than not, those insights come out of our hearts from time spent with God, and they truly represent our hearts—whether they be our own words or someone else's. Either way, letting your wife into that logbook allows her to see a side of you that doesn't come through often. If she isn't hearing you, at least she can read you. And in case you're wondering, my journal is leather-bound, worn, and the entries make no chronological sense.

Sharing our hearts with one another isn't easy. It makes us vulnerable. It exposes us. And transparency sometimes feels risky. *What if she doesn't understand? What if she thinks I'm weird? What if she doesn't value it like I do?* But when we take the risk and share our hearts with the one we love the most, we are tearing down walls of perception, walls of protection, and walls of pretense. We are, in a sense, saying, "I trust you. I let you in. I want you to know what makes my heart beat. I want you to see through me and understand me and really *know* me."

That, our friends, is connection. And when it happens, there's nothing quite like it.

We all express our hearts in different ways. And a true expression of the heart requires risk, sacrifice, and sometimes pain. But with vulnerability comes intimacy. By sharing your heart, you will find a closer connection.

Taking the Next Step

Share Your Hearts by Praying Together

One of the ways a couple can share their hearts with each other is through prayer. When I (Cindi) appeared as a guest on a television show, a man asked me about a book I'd written about a woman's alone times in life.[14] I shared with him that a woman can feel alone regardless of her marital status, and that alone times can draw her closer to her Lord. He looked at me, his eyes filling with tears, and said, "That's why I love praying with my wife. I'm concerned about the burdens she carries that I might not be aware of. When I pray with her, I hear her heart."

I never forgot that phrase...and the look in his eyes when he said it: *When I pray with her, I hear her heart.*

To be honest, it has taken *years* for Hugh and me to get to the point where we intentionally pray together. Oh, we pray together before every meal, as a family or as a couple, when we are eating together. We pray at church and in small groups with other people. We pray individually for each other and our family and our ministries. But prayer between just the two of us—as a regular part of our day—has been hard to come by. Our diverse schedules have us each praying for each other, but not together. That had to change recently. We decided we had to be deliberate and intentional about praying together and learn how to share our hearts with one another.

Kurt and Sara have been married 27 years and have always made prayer a part of their marriage and family life.

"We have found prayer a very bonding activity," Sara said. The family prays together when the children are put to bed each night, and then Kurt and Sara pray together as a couple. "Hearing each other pray and seek the Lord has given us particular intimacy in our marriage and family life."

Dennis Rainey, author of *The Secret to a Lasting Marriage,* says,

> If there is one simple ritual I would urge couples to begin

adopting in their marriages, it is this one—the habit of praying together every day…When you pray together, you multiply your joys, divide your sorrows, add to your experiences with God together, and help subtract your haunting past from your life. During the rugged times of your marriage, you can share your burdens. Prayer can also take away the desire to get even and replace it with a willingness to work things out.[15]

Trust me, men. I (Hugh) know exactly what you're feeling and thinking at this precise moment: "Yeah, I know, I should spend a few minutes each day praying with my wife. I'm not stupid and I've heard about the marital statistics. Besides, my pastor just preached last Sunday about how important this is for every married couple in the church who care anything about having a dynamic and Christ-honoring marriage that helps preserve the spiritual integrity of the next generation of Christians.

"I appreciate my pastor's confidence in me that if I start praying with my wife I'll be the guy who can singlehandedly restitch the fraying spiritual fabric of an entire country. But right now I'm just praying that my wife and daughter don't kill each other arguing over the proper length of her shorts as she gets ready to head out the door for school."

Which leads me to offer this bit of advice for both of you if you're just beginning the practice of praying together: Start with those things that are closest to home. And resist the temptation to judge the depth or genuineness of your spouse's spirituality based upon how long or short he or she prays. When a group of backpackers hit the trail, there's a general rule of thumb that says everyone should walk at a pace that is most doable for the slowest-moving member of the team. You know, the whole "leave no man behind" battle cry. So let the spouse who tends to pray the shortest set the tempo at first. (Don't worry—conquering the goal of praying passionately through all 176 verses of Psalm 119 will come over time.)

We'll admit, the scariest thing about praying together is exposing your heart before God *and* your spouse. And we'll also admit that for years, we weren't very good at taking the time in our diverse schedules to pray together. But we've recently found that as we take the time to come together before God, we can bare our hearts and be "of the same mind, maintaining the same love, united in spirit, intent on one purpose."[16] Prayer in which we express what is on our hearts (with the other person right next to us) takes time—and trust—to develop. But it's worth it because it's another way of sharing our hearts with each other.

Share Your Hearts by Dreaming Together

Another way we can share our hearts with one another is by dreaming together.

Lance and Pam have been married for more than 30 years, and they believe the key to their togetherness is their ability to set goals together and share their dreams for the future. That becomes possible only when you share your hearts with one another.

"We have always dreamed together of our future," Pam said. "We've dreamed of how our kids would turn out, who they would marry, how many kids they each would have, and so on. We dreamed about the house we would build. We love dreaming together. And if we're not dreaming *together,* who are we dreaming with?"

Some couples have dreams, but they're individual dreams, not necessarily dreams they share together. But it's the *shared* dreams—and thus the shared hearts—that help a couple walk together toward their future.

Hugh, in his journal, listed some of his dreams: to see Ireland, to own a cabin in the woods, to someday live in a home which has a study with bookcases that reach to the ceiling and a ladder on wheels to reach the books. My dream has always been to write books. Now that I am doing that, I have come alongside Hugh's dreams. I too want to see Ireland, own a cabin in the woods, and see him immersed in his study with tall bookshelves that line all the walls.

Share Your Hearts by Being Creative

Do you write or sing? Do you draw or paint? Are you a reader? Do you have a place you like to visit that resonates with your soul? There are many creative ways to share your heart with your spouse, even if you don't think you are creative.

There are times when I (Hugh) have had Cindi listen to a song that describes how I feel. Guys, this blows the doors off of trying to karaoke through it yourself. Remember the last chapter? If someone else can say it for you, let that person be the messenger. Just the act of sitting with your spouse quietly and saying, "Listen to this" will help open a door to your soul and give your mate a chance to walk in.

Maybe there's a special place you've visited that always brings peace to your soul—a place that has made you happy or thoughtful or meditative. A place of beauty or serenity. That might be a place where you want to take your spouse and prepare him or her for it by helping them understand, before you get there, that you are sharing with them a special place that means something to you.

As you think of ways to express your heart, keep in mind that it's okay to say, "I'm not sure what this means, but this is what I've been feeling." Sometimes those are the best revelations of self because you're asking your spouse to help you process your feelings and make sense of them. Then when your spouse opens a door for you, be *very* careful not to analyze it, read into it, or change or correct it in any way. Just receive it. Walk into the room of his or her heart, and just take it all in. See it as a masterpiece of art, a work of beauty that's been revealed to you. As you appreciate your spouse's heart, you will eventually come to see more of it.

Proverbs 20:5 says, "The purposes of a man's heart are deep waters, but a man of understanding draws them out."

Be that understanding person who draws out of your husband or wife what he or she wants to share. And be that person who lets your spouse draw out of you what is deep in *your* heart as well.

—— Going the Extra Mile ——

1. What are some ways you have expressed your hearts to each other in the past? Jot down those occasions here. It's possible one of you has tried, but the other wasn't aware of it at the moment.

2. Pick out a song before the week is over (or at least before the month is over) to play for your spouse that says to him or her something you'd like to say. Expression through song is beautiful, and you'll be making a memory, too. There's nothing quite like being able to say, "That's our song" each time you hear it.

3. Write a "must do before I die" list and share that with your spouse.

—— Going the Distance Through Prayer ——

In Your Word, God, You tell us You have loved us with an ever-lasting love and drawn us with lovingkindness (Jeremiah 31:3). You had no problem expressing Your heart toward us when You sent Your Son to die for us. Help us to similarly demonstrate in word and deed our love to one another, and to also bare the depths of our soul so we can be of "one mind, maintaining the same love, united in spirit, intent on one purpose" (Philippians 2:2).

Give us the boldness, Lord Jesus, to pray together regularly—not because we should, but because we long to approach Your throne together. Give us the desire and ability to share our dreams with one another and to wait upon You to give us new dreams for our future that we can discover together. Thank You for answered prayer…fulfilled dreams…and for the times You've said, "Wait—I have something better for you, but not yet." Give us the creativity, Lord, to express our hearts in a way that blesses each other and brings pleasure to Your heart as well. Help us to trust You and one another as we walk into the adventure of sharing our hearts together.

Talk More, Touch More

A man finds joy in giving an apt reply—
and how good is a timely word!

PROVERBS 15:23

After attending our first marriage conference, I (Hugh) wanted to do something tangible to remind me to put into practice what I'd learned. I'd been discovering that Cindi responds well to words of affirmation and physical touch. But sometimes at the end of the day I'm still thinking about unresolved issues at work or how hungry I am, and I don't come through the door thinking about what *she* needs. So I printed out a phrase on a strip of paper and taped it to the console of my car: "Talk more, touch more."

Cindi saw it one day and asked, "What's this?"

"That's a reminder to me of what you need every evening when I come home," I said. (Now guys, I probably don't need to tell you that I scored big time on that one.)

Our wives need our words—even if just to say, "How was your day?" or "My day was rough; that's why I'm not talking much." And our wives need our touch in a way that says, "I care about you" and "I consider you my best friend."

Sometimes when we talk, it's about us. And when we touch, it's for us. But when "talk more, touch more" is for your wife, it goes a long way in affirming to her that she is on your heart.

I (Cindi) wish I could say that "talk more, touch more" is something

I offer Hugh as well. After all, that would be quite easy for me. But actually, "listen more, understand more" is what he needs from me in this season of his life. On a day when he is wiped out, physically and emotionally, from dealing with a lot of demands in ministry, I need to let him talk less and I need to be understanding of his need for silence—or at least less commotion—at times.

Lest you think we are stereotyping, perhaps you are the couple in which *he* wants "talk more, touch more" and *she* wants "listen more, understand more." That's okay. The key is for you to understand what it is your spouse needs to feel affirmed and loved, and post it in front of you, if you need to, as a reminder to offer that.

Taking the Next Step

Can you each come up with a phrase or a reminder to yourself of what your spouse needs from you the most?

Cindi's brother and his wife quote to each other the phrase "We're on the same team" to keep tension from arising between them. It's an instant reminder that they are not enemies and they are working toward the same goal when things begin to get hectic in their home.

Similarly, at the Weekend to Remember marriage conference we've attended a few times, we are reminded of the truth "Your spouse is not your enemy." There are times when I (Cindi) have to remind Hugh—and myself—that truth: "I am not your enemy. We're in this together. We are on the same team."

Our friends, Scott and Patti, are well aware of what each other needs when the tension gets high in their home.

"Patti needs my friendship and my strength," Scott said, whether she's facing a difficult day healthwise, or worried about a doctor's appointment, or just needs understanding after a rough day. Patti, likewise, knows what Scott needs from her. "He needs my spontaneity and my stability," she said. "I'm the planner, so he likes that I know where we're going and what's going on. But he can tend to become too much of a planner, so I try to bring fun into his life through my spontaneity."

So if Scott is in the doldrums, Patti's spontaneity becomes a blessing in his life. And if he just needs things to slow down and get quiet, that's when her stability ministers to him.

By keeping in the forefront of our minds what our partner needs, we are esteeming them above ourselves. We are showing grace. And we are more likely to give them more of what they need—and less of what they don't need—at precisely the right time.

——Going the Extra Mile——

1. What slogan (or slogans) will you two adopt to help remind you to offer to your spouse what he or she needs? (Ours are "talk more, touch more" and "listen more, understand more," but yours might be vastly different.) Be creative and have some fun coming up with the slogan(s). You'll be surprised how much the slogan(s) will help you remember to remain sensitive to what your spouse needs.

2. If you haven't read *The Five Love Languages* by Gary Chapman, that's a great place to start learning about what "love language" speaks to your spouse. Then focus on the one or two areas that speak the most to your mate.

3. Reflect on the following verses and write out your insights in regard to meeting the needs of your spouse:

Proverbs 15:23—words are powerful.

Ephesians 4:32— Forgive

James 1:19-20— Listen

——Going the Distance Through Prayer——

Lord God, You are the perfect example of One who was able to meet us right where we were at just the right time. Your Word says, "At just the right time, when we were still power-less, Christ died for the ungodly" (Romans 5:6). You knew just what to do and just when to do it; You knew how to meet our great need for forgiveness. Help us to mirror that kind of love and discernment toward each other as we attempt to minister to one another's needs with just the right word or touch at just the right time.

Life can be so volatile and we can be so fragile—and even broken—at times. May we each be the one person the other can lean on for strength, understanding, companionship, and love—just as You are the One who is always there, always strengthening, always refreshing us with Your presence. Give us a continued desire to minister to one another in order to please Your heart and that of our spouse. We ask these things in the strong but tender name of Jesus, Amen.

In God We Trust

Honor the LORD by giving him your money and
the first part of all your crops. Then you will have
more grain and grapes than you will ever need.

PROVERBS 3:9-10 CEV

I t's printed right there on our money: "In God We Trust."
But do we? Hardly.

How much better our relationship with our spouse might be if we read and paid attention to that phrase every time we touched money. We would probably have fewer arguments. And we would probably experience less stress.

It's been said that married couples argue the most about sex, raising children, and money. But money doesn't have to be one of the triggers to tension in your relationship. It is, after all, just money.

Before we married, Hugh told me, "I hate money. Money should not have to dictate how we live our lives or determine our happiness. And it would break my heart if money were ever the source of quarrels or arguments between us."

Now, in all reality, there are days when Hugh likes money—when it comes in a card for his birthday, when it appears as a bonus around Christmastime, and when we're on vacation and he wants to spend as much of it as possible on what we eat. But other than that, he has pretty much been consistent in his dislike for monetary issues and their ability to divide couples.

We are convinced—and have been our whole married life—that our financial stability depends on how much we trust God rather than on how much we make.

It's really not about the money. If it were, God would just rain it down and solve our problems. But He doesn't do that. Churches are in debt across the nation. Christians are in debt personally. Ministry workers struggle to make ends meet. Yet God owns it all. He lacks no resources. So if He's not providing what we think we need at the time, we either don't need it or there's something else going on. For us it's always a matter of trust. It's a matter of where our hearts are. It's a matter of character development. It's about faith. It's about teaching us to pray. But it's not about the money.

Money is a trust issue—not just for us, but for every person. It has been a trust issue for me (Cindi) my whole life. In fact, there were times, in our early years of marriage, when Hugh would say, "Okay, Cindi, is there some way in which you're still not trusting God when it comes to our finances? Because, if so, you need to learn that lesson soon. I learned it long ago. Once you do, God can quit taking us down this road."

And you know what? Once I learned to trust God on the financial front, the financial tests and trials subsided. Hugh was right. God is faithful. Lesson learned. God has since provided and I now know—without a doubt—that He always will.

Now lest we sound like we're advocating a grit-your-teeth-and-bear-it approach or some sort of health-and-prosperity teaching, let us clarify. And we'll do this as a way of helping you get to the place where money is not something you two argue or stress about as a couple. In fact, our goal is that the whole issue of trusting God with your finances draws you closer to each other.

Taking the Next Step

If you have a financial plan in place (meaning you have a monthly budget, you tithe or give regularly to God and His work, and you have a savings and/or retirement plan), you are well ahead of most couples, regardless of your age and how long you've been married. If that's you, great job. Read on, and perhaps some of the ideas we share will complement or affirm what you're doing.

But if you don't have a solid financial plan or aren't organized in your approach to money, don't get discouraged. There's no better time than now to start trusting God with your finances. When you do, you'll gain some much-needed peace. And that will help you tremendously as you begin to put a plan into place.

Be obedient. God expects us to give back to Him what is rightfully His. Actually, all of what we have is rightfully God's, but we personally have chosen to follow a command set forth in the Old Testament when God mandated the Israelites to give a tenth of their income to God.[17] We tithe—which literally means giving a tenth of our money to God—as a matter of discipline and as a guideline of a good starting point and then add to that as we can. Why? Because a tenth is, in our case, a huge financial stretch. Because to tithe is, in our case, to trust.

We have found, time and again, that God is faithful in providing all our needs as we honor Him by giving to Him first above everything else. God has a way of multiplying what we give to Him and giving back to us when we fall short at the end of the month because we trusted Him with that tenth we didn't think we could give, but gave anyway. Go figure. We've come to see it's how God blesses those who honor Him with what He's given them.

Many times the way God honors us for obediently giving to Him is above and beyond all that we expect or imagine. Philippians 4:19 assures us, "God will meet all your needs according to his glorious riches in Christ Jesus." We believe that is conditional upon our obedience to honoring Him with what we have. And to this day, we have never been left without what we have ultimately *needed.*

Be responsible. God expects us to be good stewards of all that we have—our material possessions, as well as our money. And the first way we do that is to acknowledge that everything we have has been given to us and therefore is His. He is the owner of everything we have. We are simply managers of the money He has entrusted us with. We have found that this helps us have a proper perspective toward money, keeps us humble, and prevents us from living beyond our means or spending money on something God wouldn't approve of.

Being a good steward means that we heed the guidelines set forth in God's Word about not getting into debt, not living beyond our means, and not going into business with someone we can't trust. Most likely there isn't a couple on earth who hasn't learned some of these guidelines the hard way. We've had our share of difficult situations too. But God is not looking for perfection, or expecting us to become financial investment experts. He's looking for hearts that are submissive and teachable. When you acknowledge that all that you have is His anyway, it helps you to remember that major purchases and investments should be a matter of prayer. After all, you'll want to consult the Owner about how He would like you to manage His funds!

Be joyfully expectant. The Bible says if we, being human and having limited resources, know how to give good gifts to our children, how much more does God know how to give good gifts to those He loves?[18] We have had a great time throughout our marriage seeing God come through for us, financially, in incredible ways. For example:

- When our daughter was 18 months old, she was admitted to the hospital for four days with what looked like a possibly incurable disease. She had a bone marrow test and was seen by the best blood specialist in the country at one of the country's leading children's hospitals. Upon admittance, the hospital staff took one look at Hugh's pastoral salary on paper and handed us a huge stack of financial aid forms and said, "You better apply for every bit of financial help that's out there. You're gonna need it." (Pretty sensitive, huh?) As it turned out, our high insurance deductible was paid by a state children's service and we received two letters from state organizations telling us they were on standby to pick up any remaining costs our insurance company wouldn't cover. We didn't even pay for our meals in the hospital cafeteria during that time! God arranged for *all* of it to be covered.

- When our daughter was almost 18 years old, we began the

extensive process of searching for federal, state, and local grants and scholarships for her college tuition. We had been setting aside a small amount of money monthly into a college savings account for her ever since she was in sixth grade. But our hopes to send her to a Christian university looked slim as we perused the school Web sites and got a grip on the reality of college tuition and housing costs these days. Yet God came through again. We prayed. Our daughter prayed. She applied for everything out there, and one school in particular—the one we'd been praying for—rolled out the red carpet in grants and scholarships for her. Three-fourths of the expenses of her freshman year of college were paid for, leaving us with a remaining balance that happened to be the exact amount we had set aside in the college savings plan we had started years earlier.

- In our early years of marriage, when we were pretty strapped for cash, we would pray about God meeting our needs through the end of the week—and within hours of that prayer we would find money. I (Cindi) found a wad of cash on the floor as we were leaving the $1 movie theatre on a Saturday afternoon. It was just in time for lunch! Another time, Hugh and I were walking along and Hugh looked down and found a $20 bill at his feet. We remember just standing there and looking up, wondering if God just dropped it down from heaven at us! And we have had cars, couches, kitchen and bedroom furniture sets, and even a big screen television *given* to us by others who simply wanted to replace theirs. God has not only taken care of our needs, but many of our *wants*, too, as we've waited upon Him to provide in the wake of bleak financial circumstances.

God has always shown Himself faithful—from the time Dana was 18 months old and in the hospital to the time she turned 18 years old and headed off to college, and on many days in between. We've never seen the Lord not come through for us financially.

Trusting God when the finances look bleak can be a scary situation or an adventure. It all comes down to how you choose to respond to your financial dilemma. If you are looking ahead to what appears to be a bleak financial future, we honestly believe you are on the verge of an exciting adventure that God's been waiting to lead you through. And our hope is that you'll choose to trust Him, and not doubt Him.

Go boldly into your future with the One who owns the cattle on a thousand hills. He will provide, for He always takes care of His own.

—— Going the Extra Mile ——

1. Talk about the ways you and your spouse spend and view money. Is one of you more frugal, whereas the other just never keeps count? How are these differences showing up in your marriage?

2. If you and your spouse keep separate checking and savings accounts, spend some time reviewing how that's working. Are you tending toward unity in your financial decisions, or is your setup causing you to live disjointed lives?

3. Reflect on the following passages of Scripture and what they have to say about financial stewardship, then have an honest conversation about what you should give to God. Just as you've most likely agreed about the mortgage amount, the car loan payments, and the health insurance premiums, come to an agreement on what you believe you should be giving to the King of kings and Lord of lords:

   Proverbs 3:9-10—

Malachi 3:8-11—

2 Corinthians 9:6-11—

4. Complete a Bible study or read a book together about personal finances from a Christian perspective. What principles can you learn and apply to your own situation? What adjustments need to be made? What new practices do you need to put into place?

——Going the Distance Through Prayer——

Jehovah Jireh, our Lord the Provider:

How You have blessed us beyond measure. Even when it appears we don't have much, we realize that if we have any money at all in the bank, and some in our wallet and even spare change in a dish somewhere, we are among the top 8 percent of the world's wealthy; 92 percent of the people in this world have less to live on than we do![19]

God, everything we have is a gift from You (James 1:17), and therefore we want to be good stewards in giving back to You what is ultimately Yours. Help us through this difficult time of surrendering our purse and pocketbook—which are, at times, the closest things to our hearts. May we desire You more than money and material possessions!

We want to know what it's like to see You come through in amazing ways as we trust You with the finances You've given us. Guide us, direct us, lead us in a way that is wise as we attempt to honor You with our "wealth." Our promise to each other was that in richer or poorer, we would stay committed to each other. May our commitment to You be as strong as that, too.

In richer or poorer, we will trust You to provide all that we need. Show Yourself strong on our behalf, Lord God, when it comes to meeting our needs and honoring us as we honor You with our money. And draw us closer together as we enjoy this faith adventure with You.

— & DAY 15 & —

Simple Acts of Love

Let us stop just saying we love each other;
let us really show it by our actions.

1 JOHN 3:18 NLT

We all remember what it was like when we first fell in love. We can recall all that we did for each other, how we thought of one another. And all of those simple acts of love.

No matter how long you've been married, it is those simple acts that help keep you both knitted together in love.

In Colossians 2:2, Paul prayed that believers in Christ would be "knit together in love."[20] In other words, he prayed that a common love for Christ would have them so intertwined that they wouldn't unravel. What if we took that principle to heart in marriage as well?

Our brother-in-law, Bob, had a mother who knitted thick wool sweaters for him. One time, while she was knitting a sweater as he watched, she noticed a "dropped stitch" that had occurred about 20 stitches earlier. She was upset about that one dropped stitch and undid several minutes of work to go back and fix it.

"I asked her why she was fussing so much over one stitch, and told her to just forget about it because no one would notice it anyway," Bob recalled. "Mom said, 'Because that one dropped stitch is where your sweater will start to unravel.'"

Bob and his wife, Mary Beth, have been married 33 years and they are the best of friends today. That's because Bob learned a lot from watching his mother knit sweaters. "We are to be knit so tightly together as a couple that we don't unravel—not one dropped stitch," he said.

We can unintentionally drop a stitch by doing something careless—not remembering a birthday or anniversary, failing to be there for the other person when we are needed, saying an unkind word, or doing something rude. The list goes on and on. There are a million different ways to drop a stitch in your relationship with your spouse and to cause the unraveling to begin.

But, there are also a million simple acts of love you can carry out to help pick up the dropped stitches in your relationship so you two can be tightly knitted together once again.

We surveyed several couples and asked them what simple acts of love they practice in their relationship:

> "When my husband comes home for lunch I try to have everything ready for him so he doesn't have to get it himself."

> "He likes it when I have my hair a little longer. I prefer it short, but I'll wear it longer for him."

> "We try to sit on the couch together instead of one or the other of us being on the computer."

> "I'll do the dishes for her or vacuum the house so she won't have to."

And what are some simple acts of love a husband or wife loves to receive?

> "When he does something and makes it feel like an 'us' thing—that makes me feel loved."

> "When my spouse drops things to do stuff around the house for us—that speaks love to me."

> "When my wife makes something special for dinner that she knows I like."

For Don and Barbara, it works like this: "We both have an understanding of what each other needs. We are deliberate and intentional about doing the things we did back when we were dating—the calls during the day, a note left somewhere for the other person, little things to let the other person know he or she is on our mind," Barbara said.

Mary said, "Bob always makes me feel like he's taking care of things, and that makes me feel loved—whether he's vacuuming, taking out the trash, or fixing something around the house."

For Steve and Sophie, a young couple living in the Hollywood area, a simple act of love is making time every morning to be together.

"We have our computers side by side," Sophie told me. "In the morning, we work on our computers together. One of us makes the coffee for both of us, and we just work together and stop once in a while to share stories or laughs or hugs and kisses. We have very busy lives, but this morning ritual almost never changes."

Being intentional about practicing simple acts of love can make up for the unintentional dropped stitches.

Taking the Next Step

What simple acts of love can *you* practice?

Here are some ideas:

- Hug and kiss each other every morning before one of you leaves the house. (Research indicates that couples who practice this simple discipline have healthier marriages than those who don't.[21])
- Make your spouse coffee in the morning before he or she heads off to work.
- Clean her car.
- Pick some wildflowers and give them to her.
- Set the table for whoever is doing the cooking.
- Send an intimate personal text message.
- Ask him or her to meet you for a quick lunch break.

- Reach across the table, the front seat of your car, or the couch to hold her hand, even if only for a few moments.

- Go an entire day without saying anything to your spouse except praise—affirm your mate and let him or her know what he or she means to you, and so on.

- Go to bed at the same time as your spouse for a week. Talk, read, or share the quietness together.

- Call or send an e-mail or a text message at the middle of the day just to see how the other person is doing.

- Open the car door for her; pull out the chair for her at the dinner table; help her put on her coat.

- Fix his favorite meal without him having to ask.

- If you haven't yet learned to do this, then by all means now is the time: Put the toilet seat down after you're finished. (Yes, men, that's *you!*)

- Brag about your spouse in public.

- Compliment your spouse in front of your children.

- Find creative ways to tell each other "I love you" in code.

- Add a candle to the dinner table as a way of telling your spouse you consider the evening special and romantic, simply because he or she is there.

Simple acts of love are just that—simple. They don't take time to prepare or money to maintain. They are mostly impulsive. And over time, they can become habitual.

Cultivate a closer connection by developing *habits* out of simple acts of love.

——Going the Extra Mile——

1. Discuss with each other the simple acts of love that you've come to appreciate in one another. (Perhaps you don't even

realize how much your spouse has noticed and appreciated the simple things you've done.)

2. Read the following verses from the Bible's love poem—the Song of Songs. What simple acts of love do you see in each verse?

Song of Songs 2:4—

Song of Songs 2:5a—

Song of Songs 2:6—

Song of Songs 2:10—

Song of Songs 7:11—

3. Tell each other what one or two things he or she can do today or tomorrow that would represent to you a simple act of love.

——Going the Distance Through Prayer——

Lord Jesus, You are the ultimate example of love in action. Your Word tells us that we should not love merely with words or tongue but with actions and in truth.[22] We know that love comes from You and everyone who loves has been born of God and knows God. Whoever does not love does not know God, because God is love. Thank You for showing us Your love by sending Your only Son into the world that we might live through Him. This is love: not that we loved God, but that He loved us and sent His Son as an atoning sacrifice for our sins. And just as You so loved us, we ought to love one another (1 John 4:7-11).

Grant us the ability to lay down our lives in small ways every day to show each other we truly mean it when we say, "I love you." Knit us together in love so tightly, Lord Jesus, that we never unravel. We ask these things for Your glory and so that our lives might please You. Amen.

―――― ⚬❦ DAY 16 ❦⚬ ――――

Laughing Together

There is a time for everything…a time
to weep and a time to laugh.

ECCLESIASTES 3:1,4

Scott and Patti are the last two people you'd expect to find laughing together.

An active, attractive couple married for ten years and the parents of a nine-year-old son, they have lived during the past few months a story that no one wants to live. Yet they have laughed together during that time more than any couple should.

Within a span of only three weeks, Scott and Patti's lives turned upside down.

Patti was diagnosed with an aggressive form of breast cancer a couple weeks before Christmas. As she was weighing her options for treatment and deciding who she should let in on the news, her husband, Scott, was in a work-related accident the day after New Year's. A concrete wall fell on Scott, and doctors said it could have killed or paralyzed him. He was fortunate to have only a broken back and wrist.

"While Scott was in the trauma unit at the hospital, I got a call and was told I needed to have a double mastectomy," Patti said. "Then five days later, while I'm taking Scott home from the hospital, we get a flat tire!"

"Patti drove about three blocks on that bumpy, deflating tire and pulled into the place where we originally bought the tire," Scott recalled. "They jacked the car up with me in it because I couldn't get out. I was still in traction!"

"When we finally arrived home—after five days in the hospital—the house *reeked*," Patti said. The foul smell came from a seafood linguini that was still sitting uncovered in their oven from the New Year's Eve party six days earlier. "By that time it was a science experiment!" Patti said. "I could've lost it at that point or just laughed. I chose to laugh."

What takes a series of tragic events and turns them into a comedy? The ability to laugh—together—will help you realize that you can endure *anything*, no matter how difficult the circumstances.

Just recently, Scott was laid off of his job for financial reasons. When Patti arrived home she told him, "I had a bad day." Scott replied, "I had a bad day, too. I was let go."

Patti just looked at Scott and paused over the nonchalant way Scott reported the news. Then they both started laughing.

"Right now we can either laugh or cry," Patti said. "We choose to laugh because we know God will take care of us. He always does. He *always* does."

In fact, as Scott sat on the couch and reflected on his job loss, he said, "Well, this is a toast to the next chapter in our life."

Life can be a tragedy or a comedy; we make the choice. Scott and Patti have chosen to laugh at their current circumstances because, as Scott said, it's another chapter in their lives together.

When you are both willing to respond to tragedy with laughter, you are acknowledging that the book of your lives has already been written out by God, and He knows how your story will end. When the unexpected happens, He's just bringing in another chapter. A true tragedy would be if there were no God and life was all about chance and bad breaks.

"You have to have tragedy to appreciate the good things in life," Patti said.

Scott now looks back on the day he lost his job and says, "Actually it *wasn't* a bad day. A bad day is when a concrete wall falls on you and breaks your back!"

With that, we were all laughing.

Laughter truly *is* the best medicine. It keeps our spirits up and keeps us from getting bogged down by bitterness and a "woe is me" mentality.

"I've quit saying things like 'Why me?' and now I look at things from the perspective of 'It could be worse,'" Patti said.

That's what happens when you both have a brush with death. At nearly the same time. You become, like Scott and Patti, grateful to be living, walking, and breathing.

They have even kept their sense of humor when it comes to being intimate with each other.

"We tried to have intimate relations recently and it's like, 'Who takes the Vicadin first?'" Patti said, laughing. "And it's a lot of 'Ouch, don't touch me there.' 'Sorry. What if I touch you here, will that hurt?' And 'Oh, not my shoulder like that, move it there.' We might as well play Twister!"

The difficulties Scott and Patti have endured over the past few months have given them an amazing perspective on life.

Patti said, "Now when we get some bad news, we just say, 'That's nice' or 'We can handle *that.*' After all that we've been through, what else can shake us?"

Taking the Next Step

Yes, life is serious. But your marriage may be dying for some laughter. So here are some simple steps to turn tragedy into comedy and the mundane into something to smile about.

1. Make It Covert

Cindi's brother, Dan, works as an analyst and code-breaker for the FBI. At times he deals with disturbing matters that he doesn't want to take home with him. Because of that, he sees the value of looking for comedic events throughout the day to share with his wife, Debbie—a second-grade teacher—who does the same. This helps keep laughter in their marriage and sanity in their lives.

"Each evening we make sure we share the funniest events of our separate days," Dan said. "We make sure we both know all about the other people we interact with at work so each of us better understands the funny events that occur. We laugh and smile over our great and goofy kids, our crazy cats and dogs, funny family memories, and our friends."

Because of Dan's position in the bureau, he's often joked with family and friends that any information he has—even ordinary, everyday stuff—is classified. That makes it more fun for his children to try to figure out what he's talking about with their mom.

"We come up with funny code-names for every person we have in common so we can talk or laugh about it with some privacy in front of our kids," Dan said. "Spelling doesn't work anymore, but we still do it out of habit in front of the fourteen-year-old. He's a better speller because of it!"

Sometimes you have to go covert with the funny things you share. And when you understand the significance of an inside joke, that can make your times of sharing even funnier. Sharing inside jokes between the two of you can help to lighten the mood and bring laughter into your day.

2. Make It a Family Affair

Lance and Pam use humor as a touch point that brings them back together on a daily basis. It was, after all, what brought them together.

"The very first time I met Lance 34 years ago, he made me laugh," Pam said. "He was making goofy faces at me. That's why I fell in love with him and his sense of humor. He always wanted to be a comedian." Lance still makes Pam laugh just by being himself.

And now their son, Scott, does the same.

"Our son, Scott, has a funny bone just like his father," Pam said. "Both of them *love* to laugh together, which gets the rest of us laughing, too. It's good to laugh with your kids. That pulls you together as a family."

You two must have laughed when you dated. After all, you were having fun back then. What did you laugh about? How can those things be a part of your life today?

3. Make It a Matter of Praise

While Scott and Patti faced situations that weren't humorous in and of themselves, they were able to laugh in the midst of them. Their perspective made all the difference in the world. Patti's statement "We can either laugh or cry" is so true about many situations in life. Wouldn't you rather be laughing together than crying together—or worse yet, crying alone? In the New Testament we are told to "give thanks in all circumstances, for this God's will for you in Christ Jesus."[23] When we choose to be thankful in *all* things—rejoicing in the bad as well as the good—we are able to laugh—rather than cry or curse—about whatever comes our way. That is an investment in your marriage that will help you to hang in there and endure, no matter what happens.

——Going the Extra Mile——

1. What did you and your spouse laugh about when you first got together? List as many things here that you can think of:

2. Ask each other what can bring laughter back to your marriage. Record your responses here. Then make this a matter of prayer together.

   His desire for laughter:

   Her desire for laughter:

3. Look up the following verses and read them aloud. Then

record here any insights the two of you gain from God's perspective on joy and laughter.

Job 8:21—

Proverbs 17:22—

Ecclesiastes 3:1,4—

——Going the Distance Through Prayer——

Jesus, we usually think of You as the Man of Sorrows, but because You are God, surely during Your time on earth You also knew how to laugh with all the fullness of Your heart. It is You who puts joy in our hearts and puts laughter in our lives. It was You, God, who caused Abraham and Sarah to know laughter again when You gave them a child in their old age. You are the God who can make seemingly impossible promises come true, who brings laughter into our lives. You arrange everything according to Your plan, so when life doesn't go the way we planned, may we respond with laughter rather than tears. Teach us to laugh, not cry, at the unexpected surprises that happen, knowing You love us and, as Scott and Patti have seen, You will *always* take care of us.

May we experience all over again what it's like to laugh—together, and with You.

— ✦ DAY 17 ✦ —

Splurging on Each Other

Whatever turns up, grab it and do it. And heartily!
This is your last and only chance at it…

ECCLESIASTES 9:10 MSG

They weighed about 100 pounds each. And they cost $100 for the pair. But I might not ever get this opportunity again.

I went ahead and did it. I wrote out a check for $100 to the man at the nursery, provided he would haul each 100-pound concrete lion into the back of my car. One went into the trunk. The other into the back seat. And I drove home with a treasure for Hugh.

Hugh would turn 30 in another month. And I was 8 months pregnant at the time. We didn't have much money, and we had planned for me to quit my job when our baby was born, so we would soon have a lot less money. We did have, however, a huge backyard. Hugh had spent weekends shaping and cultivating the yard by adding a wood deck, a pond and waterfall, and a secret garden complete with jasmine-covered lattices and an arched entryway. All that was missing were two concrete lions to stand on either side of the archway. It all seemed a bit extravagant for our humble little first home on the cul-de-sac there in Sun City, California. But Hugh had always dreamed of having an estate with two concrete lions to greet people. The lions would look out of place in our little home's driveway. But in the expansive edge-of-the-cul-de-sac yard that we had, they'd be perfect at the entrance to our secret garden.

I had Bob—my 50-year-old neighbor with fibromyalgia and a limp from polio and other various health problems contracted during the Vietnam War—painstakingly carry each lion to the garage, where I could hide them until Hugh's birthday. (Guilt set in later when I learned of Bob's disabilities and the two weeks of back and leg problems he experienced after transporting the lions to my garage! But I was in worse shape than he was, being eight months pregnant, you know!)

When the day arrived, I had Hugh come out to the garage to see his lions (asking Bob to move them into place in the backyard was out of the question). Hugh was thrilled. And he couldn't believe I had splurged on such an "out of reach" gift for him.

Looking back now, I realize that money could've been spent over the next few weeks on groceries, dinners out, or a few extra trips to the discount store. But the look on Hugh's face the moment he saw that I had splurged on him was priceless.

Some couples are able to splurge on each other all the time. But having always lived on a pastor's salary (and in Southern California, where half of Hugh's paycheck goes to pay the mortgage on our condo!), we've very rarely been able to splurge. Once in a while we will do so. It's a way that we invest in each other.

Splurging on each other doesn't have to take money, though. You can splurge by being creative and working with what you have. That's what Hugh did the other night during another one of those "tight budget" weeks.

We were getting ready to watch a movie. Hugh likes eating ice cream while watching movies. But we had only enough for one of us. I conceded. I didn't need it anyway. And really, I was fine going without the extra calories. But Hugh, to my surprise, came up with a clever idea. He told me to get the movie ready and not come into the kitchen. In the meantime he whipped up a treat for me—a banana split complete with the remaining ice cream, slices of our last banana on either side of the dish, some chocolate syrup, and some blueberries. It was creative. It was a sacrifice (because he went without any that night). And he had splurged. A banana split had never tasted so good!

Splurging on the one you love implies going the extra mile, whether it be effort-wise, financially, sacrificially, or with your time. You are giving beyond what you normally would because the one you love is priceless.

Taking the Next Step

We asked other couples to tell us about the times they've splurged on each other.

Rich and Ashley save their spare change in a jar all throughout the year. Then every Valentine's Day they take the entire contents of the jar and spend it on a special date for the two of them. This past year they had more than $100 in the jar, and Ashley thought about spending only part of it on dinner and using the rest on something the family needed. But Rich insisted that the change was their splurge money, and so they had dinner that night at an expensive restaurant they ordinarily wouldn't have been able to visit. Every year, they truly splurge on each other on Valentine's Day.

Bill loved to splurge on his wife, June. In fact, to this day, their children will tell you, "Dad *spoiled* mom." The oldest daughter, Denise, said, "My dad thought the world of my mom. He would do anything and everything for her." When the kids were teenagers, their dad's propensity was probably even annoying to them at times. But today, in light of the fact that their dad passed away a couple years ago, they look back with fondness upon all their dad did for their mom. And they've stepped up to come alongside their mother, who is adjusting to life without a man who splurged in his love for her. Bill and June didn't have a lot of money during their 49 years together as they raised three children in a small, rural town. But Bill knew how to spoil his wife with love, attention, and praise. He loved her excessively (not obsessively—there's a difference!). Here's a clue as to how Bill loved June without overdoing it: He loved *God* excessively. He was lavish in how he loved his heavenly Father. And we can probably assume Bill's love for the Lord overflowed into how he treated his wife.

Lest you think that splurging on one another is excessive, we need to consider that God set the example for how to love one another—He loves us excessively. In 1 John 3:1 we're told, "How great is the love the Father has *lavished* on us, that we should be called the children of God." To lavish is to give in great amounts and without limit. In Ephesians 1:7-8 we are told that, in Christ, "we have redemption through his blood, the forgiveness of sins, in accordance with the riches of God's grace that he *lavished* on us with all wisdom and understanding."

In another Bible translation that passage reads, "Because of the sacrifice of the Messiah, his blood poured out on the altar of the Cross, we're a free people—free of penalties and punishments chalked up by all our misdeeds. And not just barely free, either. *Abundantly* free! He thought of everything, provided for everything we could possibly need, letting us in on the plans he took such delight in making."[24]

Not only did God free us from the penalties of sin through the love He has lavished on us (by sending His Son to die for our sins), but the forgiveness He extends to us is in accordance with just how rich He is. In other words, He didn't barely love us, barely free us, or barely forgive us. He abundantly, excessively, and without limit loved, freed, and forgave us. The almighty God of the universe knew how to splurge on us so we would get an idea of how to splurge, in our own little human ways, on each other.

We are also told in the Bible that God is able to do "immeasurably more than all we ask or imagine" (Ephesians 3:20). Another translation says "far more abundantly beyond all that we ask or think."[25] That is not a God who holds out on us. That's a God who splurges to show just how "wide and long and high and deep" His love is so that we'll "know this love that surpasses knowledge" so we can "be filled to the measure of all the fullness of God" (Ephesians 3:18-19). Now *that* is excessive! If God extends that kind of love to us on a daily basis, can you splurge a little—once in awhile—to show the extent of *your* love for each other?

To splurge on each other does not mean heaping material blessings on your spouse. You can—like Bill loved June and like God loves us—lavish each other with love, patience, kindness, gentleness, trust, forgiveness, and understanding. To cultivate a closer connection between the two of you, splurge on each other—and love each other as God loves you.

——Going the Extra Mile——

1. Share with one another what types of service you would feel is lavish.

   His idea of her splurging on him:

   Her idea of him splurging on her:

   (Remember, sometimes the "splurge" is in the eye of the one splurging. If your husband is not a writer, then his poem to you is his way of lavishing love on you. If your wife is not the get-her-hands-dirty-outdoors type of woman, then the flower bed or vegetable garden she planted for you was surely her way of splurging on you.)

2. This is a good time to review the Bible's description of love in 1 Corinthians 13:4-8 (which we looked at on Day 2). Look up that passage, read it aloud, and talk about ways you can lavish *that* kind of love upon each other.

3. Invest in your marriage by splurging on a Weekend to Remember marriage conference or check out the possibility of a Love Like You Mean It marriage cruise. To find a conference or cruise in your area (or to splurge by going away for one), go to *www.familylife.com* and click on "Marriage Getaways."

——Going the Distance Through Prayer——

Heavenly Father, what love You have lavished on both of us,

individually and together! You withheld nothing—not even Your precious Son—when it came to demonstrating Your love toward us. Help each of us to be as generous with our love toward one another as You have been with Your love toward us. Show us the times when an extra demonstration of love is warranted and will touch the other's heart. Help us to be sacrificial in our giving toward one another and excessive in our heartfelt love. Remind us that some things we do here on earth will last eternally, including how we treat each other and how we invest in our relationship. Show us ways to splurge within our means and be excessive in our expressions of love toward one another. Thank You for the Ultimate Way You splurged on us and the many ways You continue to give abundantly to us throughout our lives.

Finding a Getaway

GOD's my island hideaway, keeps danger far from the shore,
throws garlands of hosannas around my neck.

PSALM 32:7 MSG

How long has it been since the two of you have been able to get away?

Several years ago, Hugh and I realized that the only times we ever "vacationed" were when we visited family. Because of our tight budget, we stayed with relatives and our vacations were built around visiting family members. It occurred to us that we needed to go on a trip just for the two of us. We needed to go to a destination—only the two of us—just to be together, to take in new sights, to experience new memories and much-needed time together.

So, several months before our twentieth wedding anniversary, I asked Hugh if I could surprise him with a trip I would plan for just the two of us. He agreed. I asked many questions to make sure I knew what he would enjoy. Did he mind being around a lot of people? What was important to him in the way of entertainment? What kind of weather would he enjoy? How far would he want to go, and would he want to drive or fly?

I ended up surprising Hugh with a trip to Lake Tahoe for four days. The hotel we stayed at was the most expensive we've ever set foot in. He absolutely loved the whole trip!

Now, we can't afford to hop on a plane and go back to Lake Tahoe every time we need to get away. So we tried to find a similar place that is local, a place that feels like "our very own."

Just recently we found that place—a beautiful hotel nestled in the woods near a lake. It's far enough from our home that we feel like we've gotten away, but close enough that we can drive back in about an hour and a half. We're able to enjoy fresh mountain air, a slower pace of life, a lake to sun by, a village of shops to walk through, and even some summer concerts on weekends. (Have you noticed I'm not telling you the name of it? Because it's *our* place!)

At this getaway, Hugh has a favorite coffee shop he can slip away to in the early morning. And I have a bakery where I can get my favorite pastry. There are some lounge chairs by the hotel pool that we have claimed as "our own" and a cabana by the lake. It's become a favorite getaway for us now…where we can reconnect with each other and recharge our batteries together. We simply talk about it—like, "Hey, wouldn't it be nice to go back there soon?" And all the happy memories we've enjoyed there come back again.

Our friends Dan and Chris have a favorite getaway, but we hesitated to record it here. They love to go to Tuscany, Italy! I laughed when they told me. "Do you go there often?" I asked. "Yes," Chris replied. "We'd love to live there someday."

"That's awesome," Hugh said. We debated whether one's getaway could be in another country—after all, most couples can't just hop on a plane whenever they'd like and go overseas. But Hugh raised the point that a couple should dream big. And if your dream is to go to Italy one day, to the point that it is your mental getaway and your dream vacation, then more power to you. Just *get there* someday.

We all need a getaway. And you both need one, too—a place you love to go to that stirs up fond memories, triggers feelings for each other, and makes you smile just at the thought of it. A special place where just the two of you can relax together. It doesn't have to be expensive or hard to get to, like Tuscany. In fact, it should be easily accessible so you can go every so often. We try to go to our getaway—which has become our hideaway—at least once a year. It's become something we look forward to, whether for our anniversary or as a late summer trip before the busyness of fall rushes in. It's a place where we can feel like honeymooners again. A place where we can reconnect.

Taking the Next Step

Talk with one another about where you enjoy slipping away to. And talk about where you'd like to go that you've never been. Then start planning your getaway. When will you go? And how long will it take for you to save up the money or to find an opening on your calendars?

My brother, Steve, and his wife, Sophie, live crazy lives in terms of their schedules. He's an animator and she's a dance teacher, yoga instructor, choreographer, model, and stage and film actress. They could easily be "ships that pass in the night," and so they plan getaways—often—to help maintain their sense of togetherness. When they can do so, they plan into their schedules a weekend away together. If they can't afford a whole weekend away because of finances or their work obligations, they'll opt for an evening getaway to the movies—something they can do together for a few hours to escape from the world and the pressures of their jobs.

"We love watching movies together, going away for the weekend, and camping together," said Sophie. (Yes, this picture-perfect model and actress actually loves roughing it in the outdoors. And she's quite good at it!)

If money is scarce, try a hotel near your home that has a nice ambiance—like tropics in the foyer—which helps make you feel like you're further away. We have friends with annual passes to an amusement park, and occasionally they stay overnight at the hotel on the site.

If money's even scarcer than that, try setting up a getaway in your own home. Farm the kids out to their friends' houses, clean up your house, put on soft music and light a candle, and enjoy a date night right in your home. String up some blankets to make a hideaway (men: think "fort") in your bedroom, or clear out a walk-in closet and set up a hideaway for you and your spouse (be sure to install a lock on the door, too, if there are others in the house). Try something different. Mix it up. Go to some effort to do something special for your husband or wife. The whole idea is to feel like you're away from it all—the pressures, the phone and computer, the workload, the schedule, the laundry...*all* of it.

For a closer connection, plan your getaway. And go there often.

——Going the Extra Mile——

Talk about each one of the "getaway ideas" below with your spouse. Then, when the other person least expects it, plan and carry out one of the ideas as a surprise. (You might even want to try one idea a month for the next six months.)

- go on a hike together for a day
- go out for dinner and see a movie
- spend a weekend away at a favorite spot
- check the entertainment section in your local paper, get tickets to a concert, and go out for dinner before the concert
- visit a nearby museum or art gallery
- go to the beach before sunset with some treats in a picnic basket, a couple of chairs, and a blanket
- spend the day at an amusement park and enjoy a one-night stay over

——Going the Distance Through Prayer——

Lord, there were times when You needed to get away with Your Father to be alone with Him. And there were also times You wanted to escape the crowds and go somewhere quiet with Your friends. So thank You for understanding our need to get away with each other as well. When the world presses in and the schedule gets out of hand and the tensions rise, help us to cling to each other and see the need to get away together. Help us to pull away from the everyday routine so we can invest in our marriage. Lead us to a place where we can reconnect and sense Your presence cheering us on. Please provide for us the time in our schedules and the finances in our bank account to get away every now and then, even if just for a day, to enjoy each other's presence and Yours as well. And on those days that we just can't get away, may we find our "hideaway" in You.

Flirting Again

May you rejoice in the wife of your youth.

PROVERBS 5:18B

S ome of the best marriage advice we've ever heard is this simple: Never stop flirting. In other words, do the things you did at first in your youth or when you were first attracted to one another. To rejoice in the wife—or husband—of your youth means to never let your romantic love diminish such that others start looking more attractive to you. Proverbs 5:15-17 urges you to "drink water from your own cistern" and not from other cisterns that might look appealing. And a big part of making that happen is to rejoice in the one you married.

Yet for some reason we married couples fall into the complacent zone and think that flirting is a premarital thing that we eventually outgrow. *Don't* let that happen. It will kill your marriage.

If a woman were honest, she'd admit she likes it when a nice-looking man smiles at her, compliments her, or says something to imply she's attractive. And men, be honest. If the cute clerk at the store treats you like you're hot, you feel flattered. With that in mind, let us say this to both of you: *You* had better be the one who is flirting with, admiring, giving extra-long looks to, and sending suggestive texts and messages to your spouse. If *you* aren't doing that, someone else just might.

Monte and Judy have, for years, practiced the simple act of telling each other, in code, that they love each other. Like two teenagers sitting in the movie theatre, at a restaurant, or in church, they "touch and tell" each other all the time that they are both still the object of the other's affection.

"Monte will put his arm around me and *tap-tap-tap* on my shoulder. It's his way of saying *I-love-you.* I will tap back four times—*tap-tap-tap-tap*—my way of responding back with *I-love-you-too,*" Judy said. "We're both shy…we're not real affectionate in public. It's more fun when your display of affection is private or even secret. No one else knows about our tap-thing." (Well, now they do, but Judy said that's okay.)

The flirting gets a bit more adventuresome in the privacy of their home.

"While Monte is showering, I'll be putting my makeup on or doing my hair and he will open the shower door and stand there and look at me with his arms crossed—and that's my cue to get his towel for him, which he claims he can't reach from within the shower.

"Sometimes I'll lay the towel over my arm and present it to him as if he were a king. Depending on my mood, I might even wad up the towel and throw it at him! We've been doing that towel thing for years.

"One time he didn't know I was in the room when he was done with his shower and I caught him reaching for the towel on the rack. I said "Aha! You really *can* get it yourself.""

Another couple we know takes advantage of the privacy in their backyard to flirt with each other as they're working together in the yard. As long as they know no one is looking, they will "send signals" to one another in rather suggestive ways. "For some reason we feel safe out in the backyard so we just kind of pour it on out there," they told us. "We get our yard work done really quickly when we do that!"

Perhaps you're thinking *We aren't the kind of couple who flirts.* If that's the case, it's possible you do flirt and just don't realize it. Whatever gives your spouse the message that you think the world of him or her, and whatever conveys to your spouse that you want to be near him or her is a way of flirting.

Hugh's sister, Mary, denies there is any flirting in her marriage. "There's no flirting," she said. "We are *so* not sexy," she claimed. Yet she and her husband have ways of stirring each other up romantically, which is basically the same thing.

"If I can be that soft, understanding open person to him and he can be that soft, understanding open person to me, *that* is romantic," she said. "We live such a crazy, busy life and often find ourselves barking orders to everyone. But when we get soft, communicative, and understanding with each other, that is romantic."

If being soft, communicative, and understanding represents flirtation to each of you, then go for it. As long as you are both finding a way to let the other know you still think he or she is hot, then that's considered flirting.

Taking the Next Step

Kathi Lipp, a friend of ours and author of *The Husband Project* and *The Marriage Project*, says she and her husband, Roger, learned from experience how important it is to rekindle the romance and turn up the heat with each other—especially if time and familiarity have done a number on your relationship.

"This is the second marriage for both of us, so we realize the importance of being intentional in the support we show to each other," Kathi said. "It's also fun to flirt with each other. We have a better connection throughout the day because of it, which makes it easier to discuss the hard stuff that comes up in daily life."

Flirting also serves as a reminder that you are a couple in love, not just two people living in the same house, paying the same bills, and raising the same kids or pets.

"I feel that flirting is about letting your partner know that you still see all the things that originally attracted you to him or her," Kathi added. "Recapturing that flirt factor from when you were dating makes the reality of marriage more doable. When kids come along (not to mention mortgage payments), it's great to have someone remind you that you are more than a mom, dad, employee, and so on."

We asked several couples to share about the ways they flirt with each other. Most couples claimed they couldn't think of anything—can you believe that?! Either they didn't flirt at all (which is a problem, we think), or they didn't really want to share their personal secrets. Below you will find some of the flirting techniques a few anonymous couples mentioned to us, and we've mixed in a favorite or two of our own. (But we're not telling you which is which! Hugh is a pastor and has to face his congregation every Sunday!)

Here's a "he said, she said" account of creative flirting according to some anonymous couples, with additional suggestions afterward:

He said: "I once told my wife that I need three things from her when it comes to intimacy: creativity, spontaneity, and total visibility. For me, that was flirting big time. I was telling her I wanted her, and that was how she could be even more attractive to me."

She said: "At first I was surprised and thought he was asking a lot of me. But then I realized how those had been the three things he'd been attempting all our years together. He just wanted me to join him in the adventure. I also realize how men are wired. If my husband wants me to be creative by thinking outside the box in how I do things, and spontaneous by not being so predictable in how we approach each other, and if he wants to keep the lights on so he can see more of me, it's the least I can do to make him happy. And once I started being mindful of his three preferences, I found myself being more flirty and enjoying him more, too."

⁂

He said: "I took the risk and told my wife one time, 'You are my fantasy girl. I want all my fantasies to be about you.' And to this day, she has the confidence that she is the one I'm fantasizing about, not someone in a magazine or on television or on an Internet site. That has made her want to live out my fantasies, too. And isn't that the way it should be—that you are married to your fantasy girl?"

She said: "When I got up the nerve to reciprocate by telling him he was the one I was fantasizing about at work one day, he was all ears. He wanted me to spell out to him everything I was thinking about so we could play it out!"

He said: "Flirting with my wife is delicate ground sometimes. I don't want her to think all I want is sex. I want her to know that *she* is the one I want—her heart, mind, body, and soul. So I find ways to flirt with her that are nonsexual in nature so she knows it's *her* that I'm thinking about. I'll tell her, 'You look really nice today. Is that a new blouse?' (Even if it's not, I've gained points for noticing how nice she looks.) Or I'll say, 'Wow…you're great at multi-tasking,' or even 'How did I get so lucky as to land a gal like you?' Her smile and girlish blushing lets me know I've succeeded in flattering her and making her feel special."

She said: "When he says things to me like he did when we were first dating, it suddenly brings back that rush I used to feel when I was around him. I want to hold onto that feeling. So in some ways, I still try to be that girl he fell in love with. Flirting is so not talking to him about all the things we have to get done around the house. It's more like reminding him of something I admire in him or telling him he is great at something. It's a lot like being the cheerleader again and seeing him as the football star."

I (Cindi) wish I could say that last one was mine. But really, when I think about it, my husband (and yours) needs a cheerleader at his side more than a mother or a teacher. Mothers and teachers tell a young man what he needs to do. The cheerleaders smile and wink at him and cheer him on. Now which do you think is more appealing to a man?

Here are some ways you each can flirt with or affirm your spouse. Let your loved one know he or she is the one your heart beats for.

- Have a special perfume or cologne that you each wear just for your mate.
- Put on a favorite song or light the room with candles for the one arriving home late—whatever lets your spouse know you're in the mood to treat him or her.

- Write love notes or send flirty text messages. (Remember Day 5, "The Power of a Note"?)

- Gals, remember—think girlfriend. What did your husband look for in a girlfriend back when he was single? Someone who noticed him? Complimented him? Wore his T-shirt? Called him just to say she was thinking about him?

- Guys, remember—think first date. How did you treat her? What did you say to compliment her? How did she get the signal that you were really interested in her? If it worked back then, there's a good chance it will still work today.

- Wives, what is your husband's favorite snack? Have it ready for him when he gets home or after he's finished a demanding task in the yard or house.

- Men, make her a bath, with candles around the rim of the tub and rose petals floating in the water.

- Offer to give your spouse a massage tonight.

- Husbands, start holding her hand and giving her a kiss in public again.

- Ladies, offer to accompany your husband to the hardware store or a baseball game.

- Men, call your woman early in the day and ask her, "So, what are you doing tonight?"

When we don't intentionally let our husband or wife know that we find them attractive, we put them in the danger zone of being flattered when *someone else* does.

When you said "till death do us part" in your marriage vows, you were saying, "This is it. Just us. Forever." So don't you want that forever to be full of excitement? Don't you want your mate to have every assurance that you are not regretting that decision to love only him or her? Don't you want to continue experiencing the flames of passion between the two of you? Then keep flirting. Or start flirting again. Now.

——Going the Extra Mile——

1. Talk with each other about the favorite ways you used to flirt with each other back when you dated and were first married. Jot down some reminders here if you need to.

2. Read the Bible's Song of Songs together and act it out. (You'll know what we mean when you start reading it together.)

3. Consider picking up a copy of Kathi Lipp's book *The Marriage Project*[26] and working through it together. Kathi suggests several ways for the two of you to add some sizzle to your marriage.

——Going the Distance Through Prayer——

God, thank You for creating the passionate dynamics between male and female and for blessing them when they occur between a husband and wife. Let us never forget the importance of honoring each other and letting each other know how much we still need one another. Re-ignite that fire that once burned brightly between us and help us to remember to do the things we did when we first met so we can keep the fires blazing. Thank You for allowing us the privilege of belonging to each other, and may we never take that for granted.

—— ❦ Day 20 ❦ ——

Lightening the Load

*Carry each other's burdens, and in this way
you will fulfill the law of Christ.*

Galatians 6:2

I t was a day to celebrate.

Our only child—our 17-year-old daughter, Dana—had just graduated from high school with honors. Hugh's entire family, and some of mine, drove in from northern and central California to attend her graduation ceremony, followed by a celebration dinner. The following morning we were heading out the door to culminate the celebration with a day at Disneyland.

It was then that Hugh's 80-year-old mom fell on her way down our stairs and lay unconscious on the floor in our entryway. The paramedics arrived within minutes, and instead of a day at Disneyland, we spent the next five days in the trauma intensive care unit at the hospital, where several doctors and a neurosurgeon charted her progress from a near-fatal fall and head injury. Then Hugh's mom was moved to a nearby skilled nursing facility for therapy and round-the-clock care by nurses and Hugh's sister, Laurie. This continued for another nine days until she was in good enough shape to travel back home to the San Francisco Bay area.

Hugh was steady as a rock during that crazy but uncertain two weeks. He helped his sisters care for their mom, insisted on cooking the meals while the family was still here, and checked in at the church every now and then to make sure things were running smoothly.

I asked him a few times how he was doing. I recall getting a few deep sighs. There was much on his heart and mind. But we barely had time to think about anything past the next step.

It all seems surreal now, but back when it was all taking place, it felt as if the days were going by in slow motion. Not a lot of other things were important. No, we hadn't connected in a while. No, we hadn't cuddled in a while. No we hadn't had time to talk about what all this meant. Hugh was hurting and he was in a "let's get it done" mode. At the same time, we were working on a tight deadline to finish this book.

"Why now?" we both found ourselves asking God. Why allow this to happen before we finished out the weekend of celebration for our daughter? And before the book deadline was met? And along with sustaining serious injuries, Hugh's mother had been unable to return home at the time she had originally planned.

But God is sovereign over days at Disneyland, falls down stairs, book deadlines, and tense moments. He had a plan. And it might've been, among other things, to show two people who were writing a book on walking together how to *really* walk together!

We learn a lot about our spouse when a crisis strikes. And those are the times that truly test a marriage. Though painful, the trials we face in life can make for precious growth in a marriage. Sure it's nice when things are going great, but when all is well, we tend to take our blessings for granted, forget the needs of others, and become more selfish. It's during the trying times of life that we come to a better understanding and appreciation of the Bible's definition of love—love "bears all things, believes all things, hopes all things, endures all things."[27]

We know several couples who are going through trying times—downright desperate times—right now. A lost job. A serious injury. Chronic pain. A diagnosis of cancer. Caring for aging parents. Caring for a disabled child. Dealing with an addiction. The list goes on. And so do the possibilities for cultivating a closer connection through those circumstances.

Taking the Next Step

No doubt there are times—or there *will* be times—in your

relationship when you need to help carry each other's burdens. In our 22 years together, the glue that has held us firm has been our dependence on the Lord during trying times:

- when our daughter was 18 months old and underwent a series of tests to determine if she had cancer or leukemia
- when Hugh lost his father to multiple health problems
- when Hugh experienced personal burnout and took a year off from ministry to let God revive his heart
- when Hugh's mom fell down a flight of stairs in our home

There are more crises that will inevitably be added to our list—and yours. Cindi's aging parents haven't made the list yet, but that day will come. And when it does I (Cindi) am sure Hugh will be there—steady as a rock—to get me through the challenges he has already experienced himself.

One of the greatest gifts of love we can give to our spouse is to help carry his or her burden, or to simply walk alongside him or her during the tough times. Jesus said if we call ourselves His followers we must pick up our cross and follow Him. We believe the fact that a man and woman are made one in a marriage relationship means we are to come alongside our spouse and help carry whatever burdens he or she is facing.

So our task, as couples desiring a closer connection, is to share each other's burdens and try to lighten each other's load, even in small ways. What did Hugh ask me to do during those hectic two weeks while his mother was in the hospital and at a nursing home? Not much at all. He asked that I be understanding, that I not question what everything would cost, and that I drive over—twice—to the nursing home and bring his sister back to our house for the evening. It wasn't much to ask. I wish I could've done a lot more.

After Hugh's mother returned home, I started thinking about what Hugh needs not just while he's in crisis-management mode, but on a daily basis. As a pastor, he deals with financial pressures from our church's mortgage, oversees sometimes volatile relationship issues, and carries a spiritual burden for every person in the congregation—a burden that I can't begin to try to understand. Day in and day out he comes home from situations that have yet to be resolved or have no clear end in sight. I asked him recently what I can do, in even small ways, to lighten his load. I was surprised at how he responded. He didn't give me a list of things I could never fix, like change his job, raise his salary, or pay off the church's mortgage. Instead, he gave me a list of simple tasks I can do every day:

- Keep the house in order and the laundry done.
- Offer me a little space after coming home if you sense it's been a rough day for me.
- Don't talk about the ministry on our days off, unless for some reason I have to bring it up.
- Understand the unique nature of my job and that my hours aren't typical from week to week. I'm not trying to avoid time with you; I'm just trying to get the work done.
- When I suggest we go grab dinner, know that it's probably because it would be a needed relief for me and not because I don't care about our budget.
- If we grab lunch together during a weekday, realize that I'm still in work mode, so try your best to meet me on time.

Wow...what simple things I could do to lighten his load!

Hugh eventually asked me to come up with a list of things he could do to lighten *my* load. My list for him, too, was surprisingly simple;

- Call me during the day just to ask how things are going. (A woman needs to know her man cares about the everyday details of her life.)
- Say something that implies you notice me.
- Be willing to take over the carpooling for our daughter if something comes up for me.

- Use a calm voice and express verbal understanding when you see me stressed.

Taking the Next Step

The Bible tells us, "Don't worry about anything. Instead, pray about everything. Tell God what you need, and thank him for all he has done. If you do this, you will experience God's peace, which is far more wonderful than the human mind can understand. His peace will guard your hearts and minds as you live in Christ Jesus."[28] The same principle applies in marriage. Pray for your spouse's load to be lightened, for you to be aware of simple things you can do to help lighten that load. And then talk with each other just as you've talked with God, so that your husband or wife will know you are on his or her team.

Our friend, Chris, is committed to praying for her husband, Dan, in whatever he is going through, whether he mentions it to her or not. "I often ask how I can pray for him or what he's struggling with. Then I pray for him as I'm going through the day," Chris said.

And how does Dan lighten his wife's load? "When Chris is planning an event, I usually come alongside her and ask how I can help."

"Dan really is my right-hand man," Chris said. "He asks for a list from me. I can give him that list and know he will take care of every item proficiently. He also lets me talk about whatever is stressing me out, which I find helpful."

And of course, Dan and Chris bring their burdens to the Lord together.

Ask your loved one what you can do to help lighten the load. You might be amazed at how simple the answer is and how your efforts to share the burden will draw the two of you closer together.

——Going the Extra Mile——

1. What insights do the following passages give about carrying or sharing another's burdens?

Ecclesiastes 4:9-12—

Philippians 4:6-7—

2. Write a list of ways your spouse can help lighten your load. This will help each of you to minister to the other more effectively.

Ways my wife can help lighten my load:

Ways my husband can help lighten my load:

3. According to Psalm 68:19, who ultimately bears our burdens every day?

——Going the Distance Through Prayer——

Heavenly Father, thank You for daily carrying our burdens. You know exactly what we need before we even need it, and long before we ever tell You about it. You sent Your Son to bear our eternal burden of sin on the cross and give us His righteousness—and peace—in return. So certainly, if You could take care of our eternal burden, You are more than capable of taking care of our everyday burdens as well. Give us, insight, Lord Jesus, into when our spouse is hurting, and show us how to most effectively minister to each other in the way You have called us to. May we think of the other first, and seek to serve as You did.

—— ❦ DAY 21 ❦ ——

Keeping It Simple

God, my shepherd! I don't need a thing.
You have bedded me down in lush meadows, you find me
quiet pools to drink from.
True to your word, you let me catch my breath
and send me in the right direction.

PSALM 23:1-3 MSG

Our lives can get chaotic if we let them. That's why it's so important that couples know how to keep it simple.

For most couples, keeping it simple means dividing the responsibilities so you can save time and simplify your schedules. But for Dan and Debbie, keeping it simple means sharing the responsibilities—together.

Dan and Deb learned early on that holding down two full-time jobs and raising two children a few years apart in age means they already have little time together as a couple. So instead of dividing the responsibilities between the two of them to save time, they *both* take the time to haul the kids around together and end up with *twice* as much time together.

"We try to do most church, house, school, and kid things (sports, after-school events, and so on) together rather than dividing and conquering," Dan said. "It takes longer that way, but the stress level goes way down because we share the same experiences and spend more time together."

Dan said he and Deb noticed that the two of them argue considerably more if they're not making the time to be together. "But when you have kids and both parents work, how do you find time to be together? We do it by not splitting up to get everything done. While some people save time by dividing and conquering, we know that if we do that, we'll be dividing and falling.

"Sure, it means less time at home, but we're seeing each other while we're out and about. While it takes twice as long for us to do some things, it's time not wasted because it's time spent together."

For some people, that approach complicates matters. But for Dan and Deb, it is one way they keep things simple in their marriage and family. They don't have to figure out who is taking which kid where. They know they will both go together. They don't have to worry about when they will find time to talk things over. They know the opportunity will come the next time they're together.

"We walk around the soccer field together and talk during Josh's practice, or talk while we're picking things up from the grocery store after one of Leah's practices."

Dan said the payoff—to taking more time to do certain things— is worth it. He and Debbie get along so much better when they spend their week together. They have found that they are sharing more of their life, their parenting, and their children's growing up years together.

"We'd rather be together more and have less time overall," Dan said.

Judy said one of the ways she and Monte keep it simple is by paring down their schedules as much as possible. "We hate being overloaded with our schedules," she said. "We value downtime a lot in our family and don't want to be running here and there." So for Judy, Monte, and their two teenage boys, that means saying no more often and just enjoying not having to be somewhere all the time.

Theresa does the same: "I try to be respectful when I make plans. I check in with John to make sure I'm not stretching him too thin."

Don and Barbara keep things simple by avoiding anything that appears chaotic.

"We've come to realize that our ministry is to our family first, and that doesn't mean extended family. It means the two of us. We have to leave and cleave. So we don't let others' expectations of us determine how we spend our holidays or weekends.

"Anything that causes life to be chaotic, anything that causes a negative problem like stress, is not of the Lord," she said.

Psalm 23:2 tells us that the Lord our Shepherd leads us beside *quiet* waters, not rushing rapids. And in Psalm 131:2, the same writer who wrote about the Lord our Shepherd said, "I have stilled and quieted my soul; like a weaned child with its mother, like a weaned child is my soul within me."

Can you imagine how different your relationship might look if you lived quieter, simpler lives?

Taking the Next Step

I (Hugh) have heard it said that busyness is today's badge of success. It seems today that what really lets people know that you're going places in life is not the make of your vehicle, but how much activity you can cram into 24 hours. Bosses love it, and so do pastors. And our current culture places immense pressure upon us to perform and to produce. Now I'm not a lazy guy by any means, but I think Ghandi hit on something when he said, "There's more to life than increasing its speed." And for a couple living in the opportunistic mecca of Southern California, the lure for us to do more is even greater. Reminding ourselves that just because you *can* do something doesn't mean you *should* do it has helped to take a lot of the pressure off.

We recently saw a T-shirt that advertised—or made fun of—Twitter (a practice of posting to the world on your phone what you are doing at any given time so anyone anywhere can read about it). Anyway, the T-shirt said, "Never have so many had so little to say to so few." For some, Twitter may be a fun and convenient way to keep in touch with friends and acquaintances (and the rest of the world). But for us, it's another way that the social frenzy can complicate our lives. We have chosen to keep it simple by keeping our priorities in order: God, marriage, family, personal health, ministry, and so on. There are a million different ways we could fill up our time, but what does God want us to do? He wants us to love Him with all our heart, soul, mind, and strength, and He wants us to love our neighbor (spouse, child, extended family, friends, members of our church congregation, and so on) as we love ourselves. For us, prioritizing what's important is a way of keeping it simple.

Men, how will you keep it simple in *your* marriage and family? Once you know where your priorities are, you will know how you can best spend your time. And ladies, how will you simplify the schedule and keep from overcommitting your family so you will not get caught up in the frenzy of busyness?

——Going the Extra Mile——

1. Where should our priorities be, according to the following passages of Scripture?

   a. Matthew 22:37-39—

   b. Philippians 3:13-14—

   c. Colossians 3:23—

   d. 1 Peter 3:15—

2. In light of the Scripture passages you just read, talk about the priorities in your home so you can have a clear understanding between the two of you of how you will keep things simple.

—— Going the Distance Through Prayer ——

Lord God, life can get crazy at times. But You are not the author of confusion. You are instead the Prince of Peace, our Rock of Refuge, the Everlasting Father, our Shepherd who leads us by quiet waters. Those are such simple concepts for two people who live such not-so-simple lives. Help us to slow down, think things through, and prioritize our lives so we keep our marriage and family simple and sane. Show us creative ways to be together in the midst of everyday life even by just eliminating some activities and saying no to more "opportunities" that eventually become demands on our time. May we not settle for the good, but instead insist on the best when it comes to preserving the simplicity in our schedules and our lives. May our marriage and family life be simple and peaceful so we will emanate to others the presence of God within our home and our individual lives. Thank You for being the Rock to whom we can run and the One who quiets our souls. And thank You that Your words to us are never "Hurry up, get going!" but rather "Be still." Help us to know the stillness that comes through living a simpler life.

— ❦ Day 22 ❦ —

Disconnecting from the World

Be still, and know that I am God.

Psalm 46:10

S teve and Rhonda's favorite part of the day is the time they share together in the mornings, just sitting with each other in the quiet.

They religiously share a pot of coffee together every morning and make it a discipline not to answer the phone for at least the first hour of the day when they are alone together.

"Sometimes we talk, sometimes we read and discuss what we are reading. Sometimes we sit quietly and just enjoy the time together," Rhonda said. "It is not a time to talk about our jobs or other people's struggles or how we are going to handle certain situations. There are other times for that."

Instead, it's their time to disconnect from the world and reconnect with each other.

When we asked Steve and Rhonda what they have enjoyed the most about their nearly 30 years together, their response was, "Our favorite thing is having coffee together each morning. Especially when it's cold or rainy outside and we have a fire in the fireplace."

All of Steve and Rhonda's children are grown and out of the house now. Steve is a pastor and Rhonda is self-employed. They admit their life situation makes it easier for them to enjoy the luxury of quiet mornings together.

But what if your home resembles Grand Central Station during what others might call the quiet hours of the morning?

Then set aside time for the quiet moments. Plan them. Be intentional about it. Because much can happen—in drawing the two of you closer together—when you take the time to disconnect from the world and sit together alone.

One evening after eating out, Hugh was spent. He shared a burden on his heart during dinner, and when we got back home, he just sat on the couch. Tomorrow was a day he didn't necessarily want to face. I realized that to try to say something was not what he needed. He needed the quiet and the assurance that his wife understood. He turned on the CD player and sat on the couch and listened to music. I sat next to him and listened as well. Eventually the lack of words between us... and just each other's presence...drew us together. We sat there in the dimly lit room and forgot about the world and everything else in it. For the first time in a long time, we enjoyed the tenderness of just being with each other in the silence.

The Bible tells us in Ecclesiastes 3, "There is a time for everything, and a season for every activity under heaven" (verse 1). A little later it says there is a time to be silent and a time to speak (verse 7). To be honest, I (Cindi) don't often think about a time to be silent. I just assume it's *always* a time to speak. But much growth and intimacy can occur in the midst of silence. And you can reconnect with your spouse in ways you hadn't even thought of before. I realized recently how much of that I'd been missing by talking too much.

Taking the Next Step

Do you know how to disconnect from the world so you can reconnect with each other? Steve and Rhonda suggest turning off the television. "The TV brings in such a chaos with the noise and is a distraction from working on family relationships and just enjoying each other," Rhonda said.

Mary Beth and Bob enjoy sitting in the quiet together, but mostly at the *end* of their day. They'd like to say it comes naturally, and they try to do it often, but as busy as they are, it's a challenge. Sometimes, though, it just happens—like after a long day of work, when they both happen to be sitting in the same room and they notice it's quiet around them.

"It's usually when we're both on the couch, facing each other, him on one end and me at the other. Sometimes we just sit and listen to worship music together. Other times I will ask him to read to me from a book I'm reading or from the Bible. The fact that we're taking the time to focus on each other makes all the difference in the world, and we enjoy being quiet together."

For some couples, disconnecting from the everyday pressures of life involves getting outdoors and into the open space.

Guy and Allison will occasionally hike together on Sunday mornings before church and go up above the city, look out over it, and sometimes pray together right there as they're in a quiet place away from the rest of the world.

"We go boating, too. We'll stop the boat in the middle of the lake to have lunch and just float—in the quiet. It's so peaceful. We like camping trips for that same reason—time to be still and quiet," Allison said.

To disconnect from the world in order to reconnect with each other is not easy to do, but it's essential.

Rhonda said those investments of time in her relationship with Steve years ago have paid off in the peaceful, close companionship she shares with her husband today. "I don't think that I pointed out that where we are in our lives—having the time to visit over coffee each morning—is easy to arrange *now*." Rhonda said that when the children were younger, they had to work hard to make the time to connect.

"When the kids were little, Steve was bi-vocational and commuting, and there were many times when our 'time together' was a conversation on the phone while he was driving back home and the kids were watching a video or playing with their toys. It's not always easy, but whatever you have to do to make time for each other is super valuable. And now, with our nest empty, we find that it is the most natural thing in the world for us to spend hours sitting together talking or quietly reading.

"I know that couples who have not committed to developing intimacy with each other often discover they don't even know each other after the kids leave home. They're entering midlife—a time when many people are looking for affirmation—and because they are disconnected, they become more vulnerable to an affair.

"Being with each other, no matter what it looks like, whether you're doing something together or just sitting in the quiet, is an investment in your marriage," she said.

Steve and Rhonda, Guy and Allison, and Bob and Mary Beth are just a few couples who, after nearly 30 years together, are reaping today those investments of time made long ago.

Invest that time now, while you still have it. *Make* the time to be alone together—in the quiet.

—— Going the Extra Mile ——

Talk about some ways you two can disconnect from the world in order to reconnect with each other.

Here are some suggestions for finding your "quiet place" away from the noise:

- Arrange to go out for a weekly date at a local coffee shop to sit together, drink coffee, and read.

- Scout around and find a secluded place that would make for a nice picnic lunch together. (There is something therapeutic about being in the outdoors together, especially when it's quiet.)

- Plan some time—in the early mornings or in the late evenings—to cuddle up by the fireplace together. If you don't have a fireplace, choose a place in your home that is relaxing and serene.

- Go for a bicycle ride on some secluded trails or along the beach, if you live near one.
- Take a day hike together at a regional park or in a wilderness area.

——Going the Distance Through Prayer——

Lord, Jesus, You once told your friends, "Come with me by yourselves to a quiet place and get some rest" (Mark 6:31). Oh, may we take the time and effort to say those words—often—to each other. How we long to go away into the quiet so we can be with each other, tuning out the world and its chaos and tuning in to You and each other. Thank You for placing in us a desire to draw closer to one another. Lead the way, Lord Jesus. We take comfort knowing that, in Your Word, You say, "Whether you turn to the right or to the left, your ears will hear a voice behind you, saying, 'This is the way; walk in it'" (Isaiah 30:21). Lead us to the quiet places, Lord, whether it be our own living room or a place we can drive to and just drink in the silence together.

A Day to Play

*I know the best thing we can do is to always enjoy
life, because God's gift to us is the happiness we get
from our food and drink and from the work we do.*

ECCLESIASTES 3:12-13 CEV

*Be happy and enjoy eating and drinking!
God decided long ago that this is what you should do.*

ECCLESIASTES 9:7 CEV

Have you ever taken a day to just play together?

We make sure our children have regular play days when they're young. And when we were teenagers, we recognized the value of playing as well. But playtime can never go away in a relationship if you want to cultivate a closer connection.

Maybe you are both hard workers and you feel guilty about using a day to play. Maybe it feels frivolous. Maybe you find yourselves thinking about all the work you should be doing. Or maybe life feels a bit too serious right now to just throw caution to the wind and play. But do you realize it is spiritual to take a day to play? God wants us to play, to enjoy life, to have some sort of return for our labor.

In the book of Ecclesiastes, King Solomon, who was known as the wisest man who ever lived, wrote about the purpose of life. He said in Ecclesiastes 3:12-13, "I know that there is nothing better for men than to be happy and do good while they live. That everyone may eat and drink, and find satisfaction in all his toil—this is the gift of God."

Did you get that? Playing is a gift from God! God knows you will one day leave this earth, so in addition to glorifying Him with your life while you're here, He wants you to *enjoy* this life as well, within the means of right and pure living.

So take a day to play. You and your spouse have probably earned it by now!

Taking the Next Step

Do you need some ideas to get started? Probably not. But just in case your head is still spinning over the idea that God wants you to play and enjoy life every now and then, here are some ways that some couples take a day to play:

Steve and Rhonda, the same couple who enjoy quiet mornings together with a pot of coffee, also love the loud roar of motorcycles. "We have motorcycles and love to go for long rides," Rhonda said. "It's an inexpensive way to travel and an enjoyable way to spend time together."

Lance and Pam have always loved water sports. They live near the Kings River in the Central Valley of California and have spent years boating, jet skiing, and camping at the river. Now that they have children and grandchildren, they bring them all to the river as well for fun. That, to them, is playing.

For Bob and Mary Beth, a day of play is simply getting out of town and doing something fun. "It can be as simple as taking the time to get away to an ice cream place in Oakland," Bob said. "More like a movie," Mary Beth added. "A play day for Bob is always watching a movie. For me, I want to do something we've never done before. He likes an escape through a movie and I like an escape through doing something different."

Guy and Allison also like new and different adventures. "We have gone away to special places to hike—even when we can hike every day near our house. New places and new destinations bring new experiences," she said.

Guy and Allison also enjoy mountain biking. "Even though Guy is an accomplished mountain bike rider, he loves for me to join him on rides simply so we can be together and share the experience," Allison said. "He waits for me at forks in the road so I won't get lost. Whenever I fall behind, he doesn't mind waiting for me, and he never makes me feel bad that I am slower."

Another couple we know doesn't have much time available during the weekend, so they try to keep to a minimum the events and activities that will separate them on weekends. And they set aside one day each weekend to enjoy activities with just their family. And at Christmastime, they both take a day off to shop together for the kids.

For us, a day to play has taken on many shapes and forms through the years:

- walking through the mall without buying anything
- renting a movie and making popcorn at home
- running out for ice cream after eating dinner at home
- walking through nurseries and home improvement stores, dreaming about how to make the house and yard look better
- pulling out the old board games and playing for a couple of hours
- getting together with other couples for a "game night"

Are you starting to get inspired? There's nothing that will bring back your youthful vigor more than taking a day to play together. Consider it a form of praise to God for what He has given you. And go for it!

——Going the Extra Mile——

1. Write a list of the top five games or activities you each enjoyed playing when you were a child. (Thinking about what you enjoyed back then will help you think creatively about bringing back the fun in your lives today.)

His list:

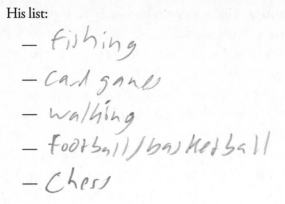

- fishing
- Card games
- walking
- football/basketball
- Chess

Her list:

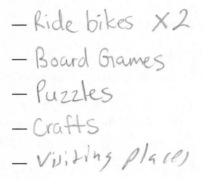

- Ride bikes x2
- Board Games
- Puzzles
- Crafts
- Visiting places

2. Now, are any of the activities on your lists an option for you to enjoy today?

3. When you think of spending a play day together, what does it look like in your mind? Share these thoughts with your spouse, then plan your next day off together.

—— Going the Distance Through Prayer ——

Thank You, sovereign God, that as mighty and wondrous as You are, You still understand the importance of Your people taking time to play and celebrate and enjoy life. What a good and loving God You are! And how we want to please You by taking time to enjoy life while we are on this planet. Help us to enjoy the little things every day that remind us that we were created to love You and enjoy You forever. Help us to take the time to play, celebrate, and enjoy life with the love of our lives, as well as with family and friends. Thank You for blessing us with opportunities to play together, and may we take them often. We praise You together, God, and thank You that "because You've always stood up for me, I'm free to run and play" (Psalm 63:7 MSG).

— ❦ DAY 24 ❦ —

Sharing a Project

*Two are better than one because they
have a good return for their work.*

Ecclesiastes 4:9

When we asked Midge to tell us about her favorite memories of "a day to play," she took us by surprise. It wasn't a day, it was a year—and her idea of playing was building a house with her husband, Ray.

Say *what?*

"Most people say, 'Don't build a house together; you'll end up getting a divorce,'" Midge said. "But for us, it helped us to discover what we had in common and it really brought us together."

Midge and Ray, who are 10 years apart in age, found out after they married that they were very different in many ways. But 14 years into their marriage, they started learning just how well they worked together when they began planning and building their dream home. "We were more mature by then and suddenly had much in common when it came to what we wanted in a home, and we learned a lot about each other." They also learned to work together on something that was on both of their hearts.

"Who would've guessed that building a house together would draw us closer? But it did. We found out a lot about what was important to us. We designed our great room together and I learned that family was important to him. Instead of having a formal living room and dining room, we planned our great room around his large family. We talked through those things together and learned more about each other."

It took a year for Midge and Ray to build their home, and during that time, they learned how to appreciate each other's strengths and reach compromises over their differences.

"This really helped our marriage," Midge said. "But again, it was because we were older. If I had been younger, I might've been throwing fits and insisting on what I personally wanted. I might've been really obstinate, so it helped that I was older and more mature."

But it also helped that they were working together toward the same goal, for maybe the first time in their married life. "Men and women have totally different ideas about building a house," Midge said. "Ray allowed me the opportunity to let it be my area when it came to design." And Midge let Ray, a landscaper, do what he wanted with the yard, and with some of the hardware and wiring details inside. Midge then said, "Things have been rekindled between us whenever we have worked on a project together."

Building a house together is not a project every couple can or should attempt. But Midge and Ray's story is an example of how a project— even a huge, typically stressful one—can be a touch point that brings a couple closer together. The key idea here is that you could both work together on something you believe in.

For years, I figured Hugh and I wouldn't work well together in ministry because we had different personalities and I tended to try to dictate to him how he should do things. But when Hugh invited me to teach a class with him several years ago (bless his heart), that allowed us a wonderful opportunity to depend on each other's strengths and balance each other's insights. He provided the solid biblical research and instruction on our study of the confessional psalms, and I added insights for application. We joked about how he provided the intellectual "man" portion of the lesson and I balanced it with the emotional, more "feminine" aspect of the lesson. We ended up attracting several couples to the class who enjoyed learning from the "he said, she said" approach. A Bible class became a project that the two of us worked on together. And I learned a lot about following Hugh's lead (and how he gave a better lead than I could've provided).

Scott and Patti, whose ability to laugh at their hardships was high-lighted in Day 16, remember some projects they did together that made for good, if not funny, memories.

"One evening when I was driving home, I got a call from Patti, who was seven months pregnant at the time," Scott recalled. "She said, 'I want to remodel the bathroom—tonight.'"

"So we did," Scott said, and started to laugh. That project became quite memorable. Scott recounted picking out a vanity that evening that Patti liked and hauling it up three flights of stairs to their condo. Upon attempting to put the vanity in place, they discovered it didn't fit because of the way the plumbing hoses and electrical wiring were set up. So Scott lugged the vanity back down three flights of stairs, returned to the store, and picked out a second vanity.

After repeating the same routine—hauling the vanity up the three flights of stairs and finding *that* one didn't fit either—Scott went back and picked out a third vanity, only to find it, too, didn't fit. So Scott and Patti finally decided to go back and purchase the *original* vanity again and just *make* it work. And in spite of all the hauling back and forth, because Patti was pregnant and Scott was aiming to please, the remodel turned out to be a good experience in the end. It was, after all, a project they shared together and can laugh about now.

Taking the Next Step

It's time for me (Hugh) to offer some advice here. All right, men, maybe you're thinking, *No way. My wife doesn't even know how to use a hammer. No projects.* Or perhaps you're thinking, *I'm no good at this sort of thing; I'd rather hire someone to do the work and not deal with the complications or possible disaster.* But your project together doesn't have to involve home improvement. It doesn't even have to involve tools. Think in terms of something you can both work on. Set a goal, and accomplish it together. Even if it's as simple as whipping up a meal together. In fact, you probably have more potential projects under your nose than you even realize. Here are some ideas:

- Work on completing a large jigsaw puzzle that you both like.

- Ever get a flat tire? Wives, that's a wonderful opportunity for you to encourage your husband as he jacks up the car and puts on the spare. And we've heard it sometimes works the other way around. Guys, if your wife is the one who is replacing the tire, you had better be cheering *her* on. However it works in your marriage, do it together.

- Do you both want to lose a little weight or just be in better cardiovascular shape? Try a weight-loss diet plan or body conditioning project together. Doing this with your mate adds accountability to the project and also makes it more fun.

- Are you in ministry together? Let that serve as a project in which you work side by side.

- Join a small-group Bible study (preferably with other couples) and complete your homework together.

——Going the Extra Mile——

1. Read the following passages and record your insights on working together:

   a. 1 Corinthians 3:6—

   b. Ecclesiastes 4:9-10—

2. Psalm 127 offers a few insights about our projects (when done in our own strength, without God), as well as our home and the projects (such as children) that might be right in front of our eyes. Together, record as many insights as you can find in this passage concerning working on a project together.

3. What kinds of projects are the two of you interested in accomplishing together? Dream for a few moments and record your potential projects list here:

4. We mentioned the book *The Marriage Project* in Day 16, but this is a great time to bring it up again. In the book you'll find ideas for projects the two of you can do together. There are even some fun projects called "Turning Up the Heat" (cooking together) and "Burning Passion and Burning Calories" (working out together).

——Going the Distance Through Prayer——

Lord, Your Word says unless You build the house (or the project), our efforts are in vain. We confess there have been times when we've launched into something without Your blessing and guidance. Lord, show us what needs to be done, whether it's a fix-it-up project in our home or a fix-it-up project in our hearts. We want You to be a part of all that we put our efforts toward. And we want Your blessing so the project will be well worth our time. Give us the creativity and desire to complete it together—for Your glory. Help us to remember that the goal is togetherness, not necessarily a perfect project. And help us to realize that our lives—our marriage—is Your continual project. We know You won't give up on us, God. It is our desire to please You and glorify You in all that we do.

Respecting Each Other's Uniqueness

I praise you because I am fearfully and wonderfully made;
your works are wonderful, I know that full well.

PSALM 139:14

We've heard it said: A woman marries a man hoping to change him, and a man marries a woman hoping she'll never change.

Every woman, it seems, wants to change her man and make him better, bolder, more successful, and more sensitive to her needs. And every man, it seems, is hoping his wife will *never* change—that she'll always be the same sweet, submissive, attractive, unassuming woman he married.

Yeah, right.

But, seriously, we do that, don't we? We marry someone we claim we have much in common with. But as it turns out, we are usually attracted to someone who is different from ourselves. And then, as we discussed in Day 4, we tend to be annoyed at our differences rather than balanced out by them.

Today, we want you to consider this thought: You both are uniquely different. And that is not only okay, but it is *good*.

At our wedding, Pastor Tom—a friend of ours who introduced us to each other—suggested that when we use our individual candles to light the unity candle that stood in between our two lit candles, we not blow out our individual candles. Yes, the two will become one, as signified when the unity candle is lit, but the two don't cease being the individuals that they are. I (Cindi) thought it was a beautiful idea when Pastor Tom explained it to us, and that's what we did in our wedding ceremony.

But about a year into our marriage, I found myself jokingly cursing Pastor Tom because when I would beg Hugh to turn down his music or drive a little slower or do things a little differently for the sake of unity in our marriage, he would respond by saying, "Remember how we didn't blow out our individual candles?"

It *is* a reminder to us today that, after more than 20 years together, we are still unique individuals with unique personalities, unique to God and to each other. And thus, the goal of our marriage continues to be oneness, togetherness, and unity in spite of our differences. That, in essence, is the beauty of marriage. And that is what we will continue to strive for this side of heaven.

Ladies (Hugh here), there are many ways your husband is uniquely different than you simply because he is a man. Most of us men enjoy some level of competition because we keenly feel the role to be the protector of the ones we love. We don't always enjoy work, but we sense deep down in our souls that Someone has designed us to be the provider for those under our care. We make friends by learning whom we can trust, who's got our back, and who will not betray our loyalty. One of the strongest needs men have is to be respected by others. And we don't take failure very well. It too often makes us feel vulnerable and strikes a blow at the core of the protector/provider DNA that's been hardwired into our psyches.

And men (Cindi here), there are many ways your wife is different than you simply because she is a woman. She will always be a little weaker physically, but in some ways stronger physiologically. (For example, women generally make better long-distance runners than men because of their level of endurance and ability to pace themselves.) Women tend to have less body mass than men, so they will get cold when you want the window open and—depending on their season of life—hot and sweaty when you feel the room is comfortable! (I can't explain that one, so don't make me try.) They will readily read instructions or ask for directions rather than try to prove themselves at something, and women have a much more acute sense of hearing and smell, which is why we prefer you turn down your music a bit and throw that shirt in the laundry even if you wore it for "only" a short time. There are exceptions to those stereotypes, of course. But you get the idea: Men and women are uniquely different from each other.

Lance and Pam, who have been married more than 30 years, used to get caught up in the pettiness and irritations of living with a person who is different from themselves. But now, Pam says, "it's about understanding who the other person is."

"When we first came into our marriage, we tried to change one another," she said. "Thirty-two years later, we forgive more easily, we don't keep score, and we're finally on the same team."

Two unique individuals working on the same team. That is marriage.

"It's not so much that you lose your identity, but that you respect each other's differences and you are not being selfish," Pam added.

Judy said she and her husband, Monte, are different but they balance each other well. "We are very different, but together we complement each other with the different gifts we have. Over the years we've learned to back off and let the other shine at what he or she does well," Judy said.

"Sometimes when I decorate, Monte starts thinking, *Ooh, that's not gonna look good,* but he lets me do my thing and he ends up liking it."

"Monte is strong in the areas that I'm weak in," Judy admitted. "I'm weak when it comes to talking to our boys, but Monte just shines. That's an area in which I just back off and let him handle it."

But Judy's tolerance and foresight have turned out to be blessings as well. For example, when their children were young, they wanted to take drum and guitar lessons. Judy wanted to let them try to learn how to play those instruments. But Monte didn't want the noise.

"I convinced my husband to let the boys try and see if they were gifted in that area. Now they're leading the worship time at church!" Judy beamed.

How are you and your spouse different? I'm sure you can count the ways. But how have those differences helped balance out your home and family? I'm sure you can count the ways there, too. Let's start celebrating our uniqueness—there's a reason those two individual candles shouldn't be snuffed out after you light the unity candle.

Taking the Next Step

Ancient Israel's King Solomon, who was considered the wisest man who ever lived, said these words:

> Two are better than one,
> because they have a good return for their work:
> if one falls down, his friend can help him up.
> But pity the man who falls and has no one to help
> him up!
> Also, if two lie down together, they will keep warm.
> But how can one keep warm alone?
> Though one may be overpowered, two can defend
> themselves.
> A cord of three strands is not quickly broken
> (Ecclesiastes 4:9-12).

In another translation that verse says:

> Two people are better off than one, for they can help each other succeed. If one person falls, the other can reach out and help. But someone who falls alone is in real trouble. Likewise, two people lying close together can keep each other warm. But how can one be warm alone? A person standing alone can be attacked and defeated, but two can stand back-to-back and conquer. Three are even better, for a triple-braided cord is not easily broken.[29]

That verse is not just a guideline for companionship and accountability so that we might live the lives God calls us to live; it's an excellent commentary on marriage, as well. Two are better than one—especially when one is good at picking up the other. Or when the other is good at making a fire that can keep both of them warm. Think of the situations you've been through as a couple. It's no coincidence you've made it this far. On days when my patience has run out, Hugh has a considerable amount left. And the reverse is true at times. God has uniquely designed each of you to complement the other. You go together like puzzle pieces. Oh, to look at life and marriage that way!

Can you start respecting and even celebrating your uniqueness? Can you start seeing your differences as strengths for the other's weakness or vice versa? We knew one couple (in ministry together, in fact) who seemed to have *everything* in common. They were very similar in personality and temperament. They were both social extroverts. They were both creative. They were both artistic. They both saw themselves as having type A (read "controlling") personalities. I (Cindi) remember asking them what it was like to live with a spouse who was so similar to oneself. I'll never forget their answer: "When it's good it's really good, but when it's bad it's *really bad*." It was the *really bad* that concerned me. The *really bad* eventually took over. Their marriage took a dramatic spiral downward. And today they are no longer together. There was no balance between them when disaster struck. Once their ship started going down, it sunk fast.

Your husband's even keel may be what saves your marriage one day. Your wife's ability to forgive quickly may be what saves you years of heartache. His inability to throw his clothes in the hamper may be a sign of his tunnel-vision focus in another area that is ultimately helping your marriage or family.

Appreciate and respect your differences. And remember the words of King Solomon. When one of you falls, praise God the other isn't so similar that he or she falls, too. When one of you is cold, be grateful the other isn't so similar that he or she can't keep you warm. When one of you needs strength, the other is there, by the design of God, to be strong for you. Celebrate that. Never snuff out that light.

──Going the Extra Mile──

1. Look at ways you two complement and balance each other by listing...

   His strengths:

   Her strengths:

   His weaknesses:

   Her weaknesses:

2. Spend some time thanking God for the ways the two of you balance and complement each other.

3. Read Psalm 139:13-16 and record your insights about the unique traits God has given to each of you.

──Going the Distance Through Prayer──

Thank You, heavenly Father, for creating our inmost being and knitting us together in our mothers' wombs. We praise You because we are both fearfully and wonderfully made. Our frames were not hidden from You when we were made in the secret place. When we were woven together in the depths of the earth, Your eyes alone saw our unformed bodies (Psalm 139:13-16). You knew all about our different personalities, likes and dislikes, and temperaments and divinely drew us together because You saw how we would need each other to live a balanced life. You saw how our differences would ultimately grow us as individuals and as a couple. Thank You that, in Your sovereign wisdom, You brought the two of us together—knowing our unique strengths and weaknesses—so that we would form one entity, a couple who is united in heart and body. Help us to see one another as the uniquely talented individuals that we are and to have Your eyes for each other—eyes that see the best and focus on the admirable traits You have instilled in each of us.

— ❦ DAY 26 ❦ —

Pursuing Personal Growth

We have not ceased to pray for you and to ask that you may…please Him in all respects, bearing fruit in every good work and increasing in the knowledge of God.

COLOSSIANS 1:9-10 NASB

One of the biggest "connection" mistakes we tend to make in our marriages is when we try to get the other person to meet our expectations for their personal and spiritual growth.

Theresa can relate. She had tried for years to pull her husband along spiritually so he would become the godly spiritual leader she desired him to be. But how could her husband possibly meet her expectations for him?

In our years of ministry experience, we have seen this scenario often: well-intentioned wives trying to pull their husbands along spiritually. And we have also seen the reverse: well-intentioned husbands trying to turn their wives into the godly women they desired them to be. It works both ways. We are generally an impatient people when it comes to the spiritual growth of our partners.

But God never made it our responsibility to bring our spouse along spiritually. In fact, in order for us to walk together spiritually, we've got to learn how to back off and let our partner pursue his or her personal walk with God.

Today Theresa says, "I've had to allow my husband to grow in his faith on his own. Because when I tried to change him spiritually to become the man I wanted him to be, it almost ruined our marriage."

Her advice to other wives? "Let your husband have his own walk with God. Your husband's personal walk is between him and the Lord. A marriage is actually made up of two walks—his walk with God and your walk with God—and that becomes your walking together."

Today Theresa's marriage looks like this: "He's in a men's [Bible study and accountability] group and I'm in a women's group. I am committed to being at home with the kids in the evening, which frees him up to pursue his spiritual growth in a men's group once a week."

Your personal and spiritual growth will not always take place side by side. But God is faithful when we come to Him—whether individually or together—and we desire to grow. In fact, when you both pursue your walk with God individually, God has a way of causing you both to meet in the middle in your quest for growth. After all, if you both are pursuing the same One, ultimately you both will end up in the same place.

But we each must be intentional about our individual growth. We know one couple who, although they both read their Bibles and pray together every night, notice right away when one of them isn't growing personally or spiritually.

When the husband is teaching a Sunday school class—which contributes to his own personal growth through his preparation for it—he notices how he and his wife are off-kilter if she's missing his class (and therefore, missing what he's learning as well) by teaching a children's Sunday school class at the same time. "Because of that, we have to make sure we're always in church together. We pulled her off the volunteer nursery rotation on Sunday mornings so we can be in a place where we're growing together," he said.

If one of you stops growing personally, the marriage will have more difficulty moving forward. A friend of ours once told us that his wife stopped growing personally several years ago. She didn't read anymore, didn't pursue any interests in particular, and wasn't growing in the same areas as he was. "I feel in some ways that I'm outgrowing her," our friend told us sadly. "I fear one day—when the kids are grown and moved out—we'll have nothing left to talk about."

Neither of you *ever* want that to happen.

Taking the Next Step

Before we got married, I (Hugh) was shown a diagram that demonstrated the importance of each spouse growing personally in his or her walk with God. It was a triangle with my name at the bottom on one side, Cindi's name at the bottom on the other side, and God's name at the top. The bottom line of the triangle represented the "spiritual distance" that stood between Cindi and me at the time. As we continued onward in our individual spiritual growth, we would both ascend upward to God's name at the top and, at the same time, we would be drawn closer together as we grew closer to God. However, if only one of us were growing while the other stayed in the same spot, we would end up farther apart from each other. The diagram illustrated the importance of *both* the husband and wife being deliberate about their individual Christian growth.

So, what are some ways the two of you can pursue spiritual growth individually and, ultimately, together?

Join a Small Group Together—Countless couples we've talked with have experienced notable personal spiritual growth—as well as relational growth—when they made it a priority to attend a weekly Bible study group together. Monte and Judy—the couple that is extraordinary at flirting together—also make the time to grow together, personally and as a couple, through a small group Bible study. (Perhaps *that's* why they're so extraordinary at flirting, or vice versa!) "We've been involved in a small group Bible study at church for most of our married life," Judy said. "The past few years we've grown a lot personally, spiritually, and relationally."

Get Together with Other Couples—One reason small group Bible studies are so effective for couples is the participation of other couples who can serve as role models for you and your spouse. But if your schedules don't allow you to meet with other couples in a regular group setting, then try to go out for dinner once a month with one or two other couples who have a healthy relationship. Chances are you'll pick up some good habits from those couples and see more of what togetherness looks like.

Read a New Book Regularly—Cindi and I are avid readers. We each read a different book every month or so for our personal and spiritual growth. And most Friday mornings at breakfast together, we have the opportunity to discuss what we are learning from our reading. At the time I'm writing this, Cindi is devouring a book on prayer that is transforming her life, and I am reading through a book on how to better develop a congregation into a worshipping community. We've also experienced the benefit of going through relationship-building books together and setting aside time to discuss what we're reading. Now we realize most people don't have the time to do a lot of reading these days. So, set a goal of reading one book every three months. Or, if necessary, even one book a year. That way, you can make sure you're growing in some way.

Try Something New—One couple we know is determined to grow together and expand their interests not just spiritually, but in other areas of their lives. So in addition to serving together in their local church and attending separate men's and women's Bible studies, every year or so they make it a point to try something new together. One spring they took ballroom dancing lessons. They enjoyed it so much they signed up for salsa dancing lessons the next semester. Another couple we know took a cooking class together and really enjoyed it. We know of several wives who have learned how to play golf so they can enjoy their retirement years alongside their husbands—and other couples.

Pursue personal growth and you'll end up growing—together!

——Going the Extra Mile——

1. There's just no substitute for spending regular time pursuing your relationship with Jesus Christ. Applying the tried-and-true

historic Christian disciplines will get you farther along your journey—prayer, Bible reading, fasting, silence, solitude, and Scripture meditation and memorization, just to name a few. Is your life lacking one of those spiritual disciplines? If so, set a goal for making that discipline a regular part of your life.

2. What instruction or insights do the following verses offer about pursuing personal growth?

a. Luke 2:52—

b. Colossians 2:6-7—

c. 2 Peter 1:5-8—

4. What can you do as a couple to grow more in the following areas (whether you're just starting out in that area, or you're looking for ways to improve)?

a. Join a small group:

b. Get together with other couples:

c. Read a new book regularly:

d. Try something new:

——Going the Distance Through Prayer——

Lord, it is our desire to continue growing spiritually in our individual walk with You so that we can grow closer to one another as we each grow nearer to You. Help each of us to live a life worthy of You and to please You in every way, bearing fruit in every good work, growing in the knowledge of You, and being strengthened with all power according to Your glorious might so that we might have great endurance and patience (Colossians 1:10-12). May we not become complacent and end up growing farther apart. Rather, put in our hearts a desire to pursue a relationship with You so we can grow spiritually, personally, emotionally, and relationally.

Remodeling the "Temple"

I beat my body and make it my slave...

1 CORINTHIANS 9:27

Hugh was watching a television documentary on the Grand Canyon.

"Hugh, I've *still* never been there," I complained. "You told me years ago that you'd take me one day. When can we go?"

"When you get in shape, I'll take you there," he said.

When I *what?*

I'll admit my first response was defensive. I work out five days a week doing cardiovascular exercises as well as stretch-and-strength training, and I have never struggled to maintain my weight (okay, maybe a little since I turned 40). But really—I was in great shape compared to most women my age. So what was Hugh talking about?

But I knew. He was talking about getting into *hiking* shape. He was implying I needed more stamina. He also probably thought I needed more experience climbing up and down into different elevation zones. Now, just because I'm not Mr. Mountain Climber like my husband—who has scaled the heights of Mt. Whitney, Mt. Rainier, and Mt. Shasta while carrying a 30- to 40-pound pack on his back— doesn't mean I'm not in shape to go on a walking tour of the Grand Canyon. But his comment got me thinking about what I might not be able to do with him simply because I haven't made a priority of getting into *his* kind of shape. I soon realized Hugh was not talking about just taking a casual stroll around the canyon rim, but doing what he had previously done: hiking up and down about 10,000 feet of elevation change over the course of about 14 grueling miles.

Granted, I have no desire to climb the elevations that my husband has conquered, nor do I relish—or practice—the idea of backpacking for three to four days in the wilderness. But getting my body into better shape so I can do more of the types of activities Hugh enjoys is certainly not out of the question—especially if it means I'll be able to do more with him.

Women can be very defensive about their body weight, especially if it's changed some since their wedding day. I am now in my mid-forties and I admit I am not as thin as I was when I married Hugh, and I've noticed the changes that age can bring to a woman's body. Furthermore, I've come to realize that keeping my body in the same shape I was in during my twenties is getting to be more of a challenge. But by keeping myself as healthy as possible, I am giving a gift to my husband that says, "I still care about you. I want to look nice for you. I want to grow old with you. And I want to be able to keep up with you in all that you enjoy doing physically."

Now, lest you think this chapter is just about women getting into shape, Hugh has a few words to share as well.

Men, it's not just our wives who need to keep their bodies in shape. This goes both ways. I know a lot of men who have succumbed to the almighty gut out of a lack of desire to exercise or a lack of control over what they eat or drink. Some men aren't necessarily overweight, but they're incredibly soft (and I'm not talking about a tender heart here). When was the last time you took inventory of your health? I'd like you to do that now. Read through the following questions and take mental note of the number of times the answer is no:

- Do you have enough energy to keep up with your wife and family?
- Do you feel good about how you look?
- Do you feel good, period?

- Does your wife still find you physically attractive? (Have you asked her lately?)
- Can you run up and down a flight of stairs without feeling winded or feeling like you're about to have a heart attack?
- If a doctor were to assess your diet, would he approve of your regular eating habits?
- Can you stand in front of a full-length mirror without any clothes and say, "I like the way I look"?
- Can you remember the last time you saw your doctor for a full physical?

Men, think about it. If you were to go "back on the market" tomorrow, would you consider going on a diet so you'd look more appealing to the female species? If so, you need to make changes to your eating habits now!

The Bible tells us our body is the dwelling place of the Spirit of God:

> Do you not know that your body is a temple of the Holy Spirit, who is in you, whom you have received from God? You are not your own; you were bought at a price. Therefore honor God with your body (1 Corinthians 6:19-20).

Because our bodies belong to God, we are to be good stewards of our bodies by being careful about what we eat; how we treat our skin, bones, tissue, and muscles; how much we weigh; what kind of strain we put on our hearts; what we are inhaling into our lungs, and so on. God receives no glory through our lives if we are not living and breathing, so we must maintain our "temples" with utmost regard.

We are also told in 1 Corinthians 9:27 to discipline our bodies and make them our slaves. In other words, we are not to be ruled by what our bodies can or cannot perform. Instead, we are to tell our bodies what to do. We are to rule them—with a vengeance.

On a recent visit to the hospital, I (Hugh) observed that some of those in the health care profession are among the worst offenders when it comes to staying healthy. But as a pastor myself, I have similarly noticed that pastors can be among the worst in the area of combining a sound mind with a sound body. Some of us put a lot of care into our spiritual life yet we let our physical body fall apart. But God wants us healthy so we can serve Him, no matter what that looks like. His Spirit dwells in us, and we should take care of His dwelling place.

And then there is the fact that many of us spend more time, energy, and money on making our homes look nice (we rearrange the furniture, replace the curtains, recover the sofa, repaint a room, install a hardwood or tile floor) than we do on caring for our physical bodies. But shouldn't our bodies be in the best shape possible—both inside and out—because the Spirit of God makes His home in us and our bodies belong to each other?

Taking the Next Step

Remodeling the temple that God lives in, your body, is just as important as remodeling your house. Here are some ways you can work toward that:

- Find some type of exercise you enjoy, preferably together. (If you're like us, you may have found that different schedules and exercise preferences cause you to work out at different times or in different ways. That's fine as long as you're both doing *something*.)

- Consider how you're fueling your body. If you *both* set a goal to eat healthier, you're more likely to make it happen.

- If you were going on a first date with someone this evening and simply wanted to impress that person, what would you wear, how would you do your hair, and would you shave (your face or legs)? Treating your spouse like your "first date" and aiming to impress—even after years of marriage—will make you more aware of your physical appearance and health. What attracted your husband or wife to you, and what can you do to continue attracting him or her to you today?

Some couples find it difficult to get started on an exercise plan, whether individually or together. But with determination, you can make it happen.

Cindi's brother, Dan, who is a full-time federal employee married to a full-time teacher, said, "Neither of us have a programmed time for individual exercise. We're unable to set time aside during the week for that. While individual exercise regiments would help make us more fit, they would also take time away from each other and the family. In the long run, we would be more stressed out. Instead, we try to incorporate as much 'family movement' as we can in our day-to-day lives. We take advantage of opportunities to walk around the soccer field together during our son's practice, walk from store to store while shopping, take the dog for a walk, play hide-and-seek in the house—anything that makes us move. On weekends, we enjoy activities such as hiking, biking, canoeing, camping, and swimming regularly during the summer.

"As far as food goes," Dan said, "it's really hard for our kids to eat at home with two parents who have demanding jobs. Because we frequently have to eat on the run, portion control is the key. My diet plan is called DELAP, which stands for Don't Eat Like a Pig. So when we eat out, I have a small rather than a large, or one scoop instead of three, or I share an 18-ounce steak with my wife instead of hoarding it all to myself. It's difficult to stay disciplined, but doing so helps make a huge impact. For that matter, if I don't pull it off, there will be a huge impact too!"

Can you each commit yourself to remodeling your temple? Do it for your Lord and for each other.

—— Going the Extra Mile ——

1. Set a nutritional goal the two of you can work on together for the next month. Here are some ideas to help you get started:

   • Eat fast food only once a week (or eliminate it altogether).

- Stop consuming liquid calories (limit yourself to drinking water both during and in between meals).

- Cut back on excess sugars.

2. Set an exercise goal for the next month that each of you can accomplish together or individually. We gave you ideas for the nutritional goal; try to come up with your own ideas for getting the exercise you need:

—Going the Distance Through Prayer—

Lord God, our Creator and Sustainer:

Be at home in our bodies, Your dwelling place. May we clean out every corner of our heart, mind, and soul that is not fit for a King, and give You only the best through our care and keeping of Your temple. Help us to make wise choices when it comes to staying active and fueling our bodies with energy-inducing foods. We want to be healthy representatives of You and Your kingdom by maintaining a right balance between body, mind, and soul. May we not neglect our outer, physical bodies in our endeavor to be spiritually healthy, and may we not neglect our inner spiritual selves in our effort to be physically healthy. Keep us active, God, so that we are able to continue serving You even in our senior years. Help us to discipline ourselves to stay healthy so we can give each other our best, keeping in mind that our bodies belong not only to You, but to each other. Lord, may our buffeting our body and making it our slave be a spiritual form of worship to You. And may we ultimately bless each other too.

Having a Mission

We are God's workmanship, created in
Christ Jesus to do good works,
which God prepared in advance for us to do.

EPHESIANS 2:10

S o why did God bring the two of you together anyway? As you think about your life together, what is your mission as a couple? What does God want to accomplish through both of you that He has chosen not to do with just one of you?

We believe every couple must ask those questions: *Why are we together? What is our purpose, and how can we fulfill it together?* A marriage must be about more than your corporate or individual happiness. It must be about more than just your love for each other. And as Hugh would say, "Your marriage needs to be about a lot more than just playing house and making sure the kitchen towels always match the curtains."

When we got engaged, we agreed upon a verse for our wedding invitation. We felt it appropriate to announce to our family and friends the bigger purpose behind why we were getting married. Yes, we were in love. Yes, we wanted to spend the rest of our days together and raise a family and leave a legacy. But beyond that we were two individuals who loved God with all our hearts. And whether we were married or not, we knew we'd be serving God. It made sense, then, that God brought us together so we could serve Him even more effectively.

The verse we placed on our wedding invitation was Psalm 34:3:

"O magnify the LORD with me, and let us exalt His name together."[30] That truly was our goal as a couple—to exalt God's name throughout our lives together. We didn't know exactly what that would look like, so we continued to serve God in the capacity that we had before our marriage. I continued to disciple women, which has since led to a national speaking ministry and the publication of several books for women. Hugh, who was a Bible student set on becoming a pastor, has served as an associate and senior pastor of churches over the past 20 years, trained leaders, discipled men, and spearheaded ministries in evangelism, children's education, community outreach, and lay counseling. Eventually we saw how God wanted us to serve Him *together* and we've been able to teach Bible classes together, train leaders, and minister to couples. Now, by God's grace, we are writing books for couples.

You might be thinking, *Well, you're in full-time ministry; that's your job.* But as followers of Christ, serving the Lord is *your* job too. You can both work actively for the Lord no matter what your vocation. The manner in which you do your job and interact with your coworkers has the potential to call attention to and bring glory to God.

Jesus said the greatest commandment is to love the Lord your God with all your heart, soul, mind, and strength, and He said the second greatest commandment is to love your neighbor as yourself (Matthew 22:37-39). As you and your spouse love God and others, ministry will happen.

Maybe your mission is to open your home so you can reach your children's friends. Back on Day 8 ("Taking a Walk"), we talked about Cindi's Uncle Owen and Aunt Alice, who have been married more than 50 years and are relishing their retirement years together. Back when Cindi was young, Owen and Alice lived out a mission in their home, even if they didn't see it at the time. Their home was a refuge, the kind of place you'd want to go to on Sundays for dinner. It was the one house where all the kids' friends wanted to hang out most of the time.

Later, when Owen and Alice's oldest son, Mark, was in college, he led a Bible study in his parents' home. Every week, Owen and Alice would open their house for anywhere from five to fifteen kids. They would sit in the living room, hang around the kitchen, and talk in the front yard, staying late into the night.

"When Mark had his Bible study here and had all these kids coming over to study the Bible, it kept us younger," Owen said. "We still hear from some of those kids today."

When Mark passed away in his early forties, the memorial service was packed with adults who shared, one after the other, how they grew spiritually through the Bible studies and through the "warmth of Mark's home" and the "ministry of Mark's parents." Story after story, testimony after testimony alluded to the impact that "Mark's parents" had had on these college kids, many of whom became leaders in their homes and churches. One of the nurses who cared for Mark while he was in a coma during the last few days of his life happened to be a young woman who had at one time sat in Owen and Alice's living room and attended Mark's Bible study.

Mark's sister, Tami, said, "She was present when Mark died, and she helped at his memorial service. When I saw her recently she said, 'My mom suffered from depression when I was growing up and I never really felt like I had a mom. Your mom was like a mom to me.'"

Owen and Alice may not have set out for their home to serve as a mission outreach to their children's friends, but God engineered it that way.

Perhaps that's *your* mission right now: to raise your children—or your grandchildren—in the love and fear of the Lord.

Bob and Mary Beth readily responded that their mission is "to serve the body of Christ." They have made serving in their church something they have always done together.

"In our local church, we've been called to help them in *whatever* they ask us to do. And I mean *whatever*," Mary Beth said. "At church, Bob and I work really well together. I can't imagine what our lives would be like if we weren't serving together."

Kurt and Sara, a ministry couple who have been married 27 years, have been on cross-cultural missions trips together, and Sara said those trips "always turn out to be as good for us as they are for the people we're loving and serving in the name of Christ."

Sara added that she and Kurt also realized early on that their mission to their two adopted children was to teach them to pray. And this pastor and his wife have succeeded in leaving their children a legacy of prayer.

Sara recently told us, "Our daughter, Lauren, has recently married and told us of how she and her husband, Zach, are making a habit of praying every night when they go to bed. You can imagine how blessed we were to hear how this tradition, which has helped bond us as a family, is now being passed down to the next generation."

And our friends Steve and Rhonda have a cottage home in northern California that they open as a hideaway and safe retreat for other couples in ministry who need a chance to get away together. It has become their mission to reach out to other pastors, like Steve, and their wives, like Rhonda, who need some quiet time to reconnect with each other so they can return home refueled and refreshed, ready to serve others.

All the couples we just mentioned married for love. Yet they also shared a love for God, and wanted to be used by Him for His glory. By loving God and wanting to serve Him and His people, they found their mission in life—together.

Taking the Next Step

What is God's mission for *your* marriage? It starts with who you are and where God has placed you. What is unique about the two of you? Who enjoys spending time around you both? What people, events, interests, or opportunities keep showing up in your life that convince you that God is up to something? As you begin to think about the people who are affected by your lives and your marriage, you will begin to see the bigger picture in which God has placed you. And you will begin to catch the excitement that sets in when you realize your marriage really is about more than just the two of you.

Begin praying about that mission God has given you. If you don't know what it is yet, pray about that too. Ask God to make it clear and to confirm it to you. Pray about it individually and together. And then tell God you're ready to go out and conquer—together. There is nothing more exciting than being married and on a mission for God.

——Going the Extra Mile——

1. Think back upon the circumstances that brought the two of you together. What forces were at work that caused the two of you to consider a life together?

2. What type of service for God's kingdom would you desire to do that can only be accomplished alongside your spouse?

3. Identify each of your spiritual gifts, then look at how they complement each other. How can they be used together in ministry to others?

4. Meet with another couple who is serving God together and ask them how they function as partners in ministry. How did they get started? How did they clarify their mission? How do they share the ministry tasks and goals that are before them?

——Going the Distance Through Prayer——

Maker of Our Souls:

Certainly You had a plan for the two of us when You brought us together. Your Word says we are Your workmanship, created in Christ Jesus to do good works, which You prepared in advance for us to do (Ephesians 2:10). Show us, specifically, what our mission is so we can do those good works You prepared long ago for us to accomplish for Your glory. Please open our eyes to see the people whom You have strategically placed in our lives for ministry purposes. Lead us into a servant mode so we will not miss any opportunity You bring our way to help others and impact their lives for eternity. May we never underestimate what You might desire to do through us. We consider it a privilege, God, to be on mission for you. May we always see our marriage as an arena through which You can, in some way, build the kingdom of God.

When Troubles Loom Large

*The LORD is a refuge for the oppressed,
a stronghold in times of trouble.*

PSALM 9:9

*The LORD is my light and my salvation—whom shall I fear?
The LORD is the stronghold of my life—
of whom shall I be afraid?*

PSALM 27:1

There are troubles in marriage relationships, and then there are *little foxes*. It's important for us to know the difference between the two.

In this book we've talked about extending grace to our partner, who is as much of a sinner as we are. We've addressed seeing the good, not the bad, in them and praising the positive. But now it's time to address the pesky issues that can bring trouble. For when you know what to watch for, you're less likely to suffer serious harm in your marriage.

In the Bible is a beautiful line of poetry that acknowledges the irritations, problems, and differences that can surface in any intimate relationship. In this poem, a bride is singing the praises of her beloved husband when her brothers offer some advice about keeping the romance alive and their hearts continually fixed on each other: "Catch for us the foxes, the little foxes that ruin the vineyards, our vineyards that are in bloom" (Song of Songs 2:15).

"The little foxes" is a metaphor for the kinds of problems that can disturb or destroy a relationship. The well-meaning brothers in this song wanted their sister to be rid of anything that could potentially hurt the relationship between the newlyweds (just like vineyards must be free of "little foxes" that can wreak havoc among the vines). Many times it is the little foxes that, when ignored or trivialized, will end up causing the biggest problems in a marriage.

Every couple can identify their little foxes. What annoys you, spoils a mood, or stirs you to become frustrated with your spouse? What is spoiling the vines? We covered some possible little foxes in the chapters "Praising the Positive" and "Extending Grace."

The foxes, however, are not the real threat. Oh, if only the little foxes were all we had to worry about! If only there were no bigger beasts to fear. But, in fact, there is a lion lurking out there as well. And he's more trouble than anything the little foxes can conjure up.

Because they are small, we can deal with the foxes. In fact, the foxes run from us. The lion, however, is *hunting* us.

We (husbands and wives included) are given this warning in the Bible: "Be on your guard and stay awake. Your enemy, the devil, is like a roaring lion, sneaking around to find someone to attack" (1 Peter 5:8 CEV).

In another Bible translation that verse says, "Your enemy the devil prowls around like a roaring lion looking for someone to devour."[31] That means you and your marriage are on Satan's list of things to devour. Do you realize that? Sometimes he'll strike at you, or your spouse, in order to take down the marriage. Or he may start with the marriage in order to take out the two of you. That's why we're told to be *alert.* If we know he's out there and what he's up to, we won't be as likely to succumb to his wiles.

There are times when Hugh and I have to remind ourselves that there is a lion prowling about us, seeking one or both of us for lunch! (In our case, it's usually dinner, as he often chooses that time of the day to strike—when we're hungry, tired, and feeling worn out and defeated from various battles throughout the day.)

Before we share with you the strategy the Bible gives for dealing with this lion, let us give some insight on *why* you are both a target.

Marriage is an institution ordained by God. No other relationship better portrays the kind of love God has for us than that of a committed husband willing to lay down his life for his bride. In fact, God calls His followers His "bride," and Scripture talks of a coming wedding feast and "marriage supper of the Lamb" when Christ is reunited with His bride, the church. Because of the power that a godly marriage has to mirror the love and commitment of Christ to His church, it will inevitably come under attack. And the more potential you and your spouse have of mirroring the love Christ has for His church, the more fierce the attack might be.

Now, we're not saying that every problem in a marriage is an attack from Satan. The fact that a marriage brings together two people with different personalities, temperaments, preferences, and opinions can ignite enough sparks to start a wildfire. There are enough explosives in a marriage just from the combined dysfunctions, idiosyncrasies, and sinful tendencies of each partner. But there are also times when the enemy—or his minions—is clearly at work. You can't hear his roar, but you know something isn't quite right. Satan is on the prowl. And trouble's coming.

In our experience, we've narrowed it down to situations in which we can't put our finger on anything else. Times when he can't be seen or heard but his dark and vicious presence can be felt. Have you ever experienced...

- A conversation that suddenly turns south and your partner claims you said things that you honestly didn't say? (Or at least, that's how he or she heard it?)

- A confusion and irritability that you can't really attribute to anything else?

- A type of tension in the air and it seems like nothing can be said on either end to cut through it?

- An accusation in your mind about your spouse, but you're not sure where it's coming from?

- A nagging thought that you aren't loved or respected by your partner, so why should you love or respect him or her in return?

- Some past offense by your spouse that is thrust to the forefront of your mind?

- Any thought about your spouse that is not true, noble, right, pure, lovely, or admirable? [32]

As a couple in a ministry marriage—that is, we are both involved in full-time ministry—we have seen firsthand how the enemy wishes to divide us and pull us down. If he can take down a pastor's marriage, he can take down a whole church with it. There is much at stake in our marriage. There is much at stake in *yours*, too.

The enemy will taunt each of you, separately, with the ideas that your happiness is important, that you'd be happier or better off without each other, that God would rather have you happy and divorced than unhappily married. Every one of those ideas is a lie from the pit of hell. And they need to stay there.

Your marriage affects not only the two of you but your children, your grandchildren (if you have any), your immediate family, your friends, your personal well-being, your emotional and physical health (those who stay together for life, on average, live longer), and more.

This morning I (Cindi) woke up battle-weary. I knew Hugh was just as weary. I could see it on his face. The onslaught from the enemy has been fierce as we've battled through writing this book. But when troubles loom large, when the enemy appears powerful, that's when God shows Himself stronger on our behalf.

God's words to us are the same as they were to the apostle Paul, who was being tried and tested with some buffeting from Satan when he wrote the following: "My grace is sufficient for you, for my power is made perfect in weakness." And Paul's response was, "Therefore...I delight in weaknesses, in insults, in hardships, in persecutions, in difficulties. For when I am weak, then I am strong" (2 Corinthians 12:9-10).

Those verses got me (Cindi) to thinking: When we're weak and we admit we're helpless in the battle, that's when God takes over and shows Himself strong. Our battle gives God a chance to show up and reveal what He can do!

One morning I found myself praying, "God, take me out of the battle. Let this *stop*." That's when I realized that as long as our marriage is a threat to the kingdom of darkness, it will be assaulted by unseen forces. It's when we get complacent and wrapped up in ourselves to the point that we're offering nothing good to anyone else that we move from threat status to status quo. It's probably then that the enemy thinks, *They're having enough trouble on their own; I can take a break from them for awhile. I'll find a marriage that's really making a difference and go after* that *one*. Oh, may that never be the case with us... or with you!

This morning, instead of praying to be relieved from the battle altogether, we thanked God for the opportunity to be considered battleworthy, and prayed for protection in the midst of it. Now that's not a bad thing to do on a regular basis—whether you're writing a book on marriage or not!

So because we're in this battle, we must know, without a doubt, how to suit up and be prepared.

Taking the Next Step

Scripture gives us detailed instruction in how to suit up to defeat the lion that seeks to devour us. In fact, God's Word calls us to put on the armor that is essential for the unseen battles you will face not only in life and at work, but in your marriage as well.

We are told in Ephesians 6:10-17 to be strong in the Lord and put on the "full armor of God" so that we can take our stand against the devil's schemes. Our struggle is "not against flesh and blood," but against the powers of darkness and "against the spiritual forces of evil in the heavenly realms." We are to put on the belt of truth, the breastplate of righteousness, the shield of faith, the helmet of salvation, and the sword of the Spirit—all that we might stand firm.

If you pay close attention to what the passage says, you will realize that putting on the armor of God is nothing less than adorning yourself in the character of Jesus Christ. Each piece of the armor makes reference to an aspect of Christ's nature or character. So when we are told to stand firm with the belt of truth buckled around our waist, we can know confidently that at the core of our being should be Jesus—who is the truth, as described in John 14:6. When we are told to put on the breastplate of righteousness, we are being told to clothe ourselves in Christ, who is called "The LORD our Righteousness" in Jeremiah 23:6. Our helmet of salvation is Christ, again, because salvation is found in no other name (Acts 4:12). So as you go through the process of "suiting up," keep in mind that as a couple you are not fighting your battles alone. You can recruit the supernatural power of the Son of God as you face the lion who wants to devour you.

So no matter what Satan brings to the battle, we have the Son of God fighting on our behalf. With Him at our side, we have no reason to fear. Together, we are poised for battle and we are standing firm. As Scripture says, a cord of three strands (you, your spouse, and the Lord fighting on your behalf) is not easily broken.[33]

So suit up and stand firm. When troubles loom large, your God, wielding His sword on your behalf, looms larger!

—— Going the Extra Mile ——

1. Talk about the "little foxes" that might attempt to wreak havoc on your marriage. How can you best be aware that that is all they are—pesky little foxes?

2. Talk with your spouse about coming up with a phrase or code word that you can use to alert each other when you sense that you are under spiritual attack in your marriage.

3. Read Ephesians 6:10-17. Below are listed the various parts of the armor you're to put on for spiritual battle. Next to each article of armor is a corresponding Bible passage that shows Christ as the armor piece. After each one, write a few words about what this piece of armor means for your marriage, or what it means for you each to be "clothed" in Christ in that area:

Verse 14: the belt of truth (Isaiah 11:5)—

Verse 14: the breastplate of righteousness (Isaiah 59:17)—

Verse 15: feet shod with the readiness of the gospel (Isaiah 52:7)—

Verse 16: the shield of faith (Psalm 91:4)—

Verse 17: the helmet of salvation (Isaiah 59:17)—

Verse 17: the sword of the Spirit, which is the Word of God (Revelation 1:16)—

——Going the Distance Through Prayer——

Use this prayer, based on Ephesians 6:10-17, as a way of "putting on the armor of God" to protect your marriage:

Lord God, our Warrior and Defender:

We so need Your help to be strong in this battle that ensues around us. Help us to be strong, together, in You and in Your mighty power. Clothe us in the full armor of God so we can take our stand against the devil's schemes. We know our struggle is not against each other or anyone else, but against the rulers, against the authorities, against the powers of this dark world and against the spiritual forces of evil in the heavenly realms. Therefore, we put on the full armor of God, so that we may be able to stand our ground. Help us to stand firm with the belt of truth buckled around our waist, as we acknowledge that You, Lord Jesus, are the way, the truth, and the life (John 14:6). Help us to stand, as well, with the breastplate of righteousness in place, knowing You are the Lord our Righteousness (Isaiah 45:24). And may our feet be fitted with the readiness that comes from the gospel of peace, and You, O Lord, are Jehovah Shalom, the Lord our Peace. In addition to this, we take up the shield of faith, knowing the Lord God is a shield (Psalm 84:11) and our faith is found in no other name than Jesus. With this shield we will be able to extinguish the flaming arrows of the evil one. Finally, we take the helmet of salvation, knowing that salvation is found in no other name than Jesus, as well as the sword of the Spirit, which is the Word of God. You, Lord Jesus, are the Word (John 1:1).

Fully clothed in You, covered in Your righteousness and Your salvation, we stand firm against any efforts by the evil one to come against us. We thank You and praise You for the victory we have in Christ Jesus. Amen.

When the Path
Looks Impossible

*Jesus replied, "What is impossible with
men is possible with God."*

LUKE 18:27

Our hearts broke when we received the call.
    Some friends of ours had been experiencing difficulty in their
marriage. Real difficulty. For the past few years. The kinds of things that
are tough at first, then go from bad to worse. He was making bad decisions. She was feeling more and more like a victim. Trust between them
was eroding away. Unconditional love was on the line. There were seemingly fewer and fewer reasons for them to stay together, apart from unconditional love—which, of course, is what marriage is ultimately made of.

Yet the phone call this morning let us know that she had filed for
divorce. As far as she was concerned, the marriage was over. As far as
he was concerned, his life was over.

I suppose we saw it coming. We knew she was determined to be free
of the disaster he was continuing to wreak upon their lives. We knew, too,
that she had been through so much already. She, in many ways, felt this
was the only decision she could make for her well-being and that of her
children. She, too, never believed it would come to this. Neither did we.

In our 20 years of ministry together, we've seen situations that
looked impossible. But we also know the God of the impossible. We've
seen unhealthy marriages that were written off to die. But we also
know the One who is called the Resurrection and the Life,[34] the Great

Physician, and the Lord our Healer.[35] Scripture says nothing is too difficult for Him. We've seen marriages that looked absolutely unworkable. And then God showed up and held the couple together as He holds the galaxies in His hand.

When couples throw in the towel, they are saying, in a sense, "Not even God can fix this." "Not even God can redeem this situation." "Not even God can change his [or her] heart." Those are dangerous statements to make, for "with God all things are possible."[36]

Dear friends, if you are ever tempted to believe your marriage is unworkable, we ask you—we *beg* you—to turn it over to the One who can heal the sick, cause the blind to see, and raise the dead to life. He wants your marriage to endure the test of time even more than you do. So don't give up on Him. You may, at times, feel like giving up on your spouse, or you may someday come to a point in your marriage where you no longer believe in your spouse. But don't ever give up on the Lord Jesus Christ, who can hold all things together. Never quit believing in what He can do. As long as each of you commits to never giving up on God and what He can do, then you'll never give up on your marriage either. It's when we say, "This is unfixable" that we are really saying, "God can no longer fix this."

Isn't it interesting that we will readily believe that Jesus Christ's death on the cross paid the penalty for our sin and delivered us from eternal judgment and damnation, yet we have trouble believing that same God who saved our soul can also save our marriage? We trust Him for our eternal life, but not in our everyday life. Isn't that a stark contradiction in terms?

Certainly if He can secure our eternal salvation, He can secure our marriage vows and keep our relationship together. Certainly if He can take care of our eternal destiny, He can take care of our earthly commitment in marriage. The problem is that we tend to expect our *spouse* to come through when there are troubles, rather than God. We expect our husband or wife to change, when only God can work transformation in an individual and in a marriage. We tend to believe a marriage rises and falls on how much we can trust a *person,* rather than on how much we can trust God.

As we said in the last chapter, God ordained marriage. It is an institution to Him that is holy and set apart. He will fight for it. Will you?

In their book *Love and War,* John and Stasi Eldredge say the most compelling reason to stay married—to continue to choose love rather than the alternative—is to have more of God. They say that to stay married because you hope the other person will eventually change is not enough. For your spouse might not change. They say that to stay together because you made a vow and you want to keep it and be a person of integrity is commendable. But to stay together because you *must* (and not solely because your heart is in it) is not what God intended. Staying together because you want to be a person who is true to your word and becomes what God wants you to be is a better answer.

Ultimately, you want to stay together because you want to have more of God. To choose to love because that is what we were created to do—to love God and love others—is the highest calling. God's greatest commandment is for us to love Him with all our heart, soul, mind, and strength, and His second greatest commandment is for us to love our neighbor as ourselves. And those two commands go together. We can't love God with all of our being yet choose not to love our spouse because life is just too painful if we do. We can't love God with all that we are and say, "My personal growth and well being is more important than my vow to God and to my spouse." We can't love God with all our heart, soul, mind, and strength without sacrificially loving the one God brought into our life for us to love *till death do us part.*

In the words of John and Stasi Eldredge: "Every time we choose to love, we take a step closer to God; it is like he is right there. Every time we choose something else, we take a step away."[37]

I (Cindi) experienced the ravages of divorce when my parents split up after 22 years of marriage. Divorce, I was told, was not an option in a Christian marriage. But it eventually became the option one of my parents chose. Although both of my parents are remarried today, my sister and brothers and I still live with that pocket of pain in our hearts of what could've been. God redeems. He restores. He has healed all of us—my parents included. But He wasn't given the chance to heal and redeem them…before divorce delivered the final blow. (Actually, how I *wish* it had been the final blow. But in many ways divorce is the first of many blows in having to deal with the aftermath of the dissolution of a marriage—whether your parents', your children's, or your own.) And thus I grew up seeing the kind of marriage I *didn't* want to have. I saw a choice made by my parents that I never want to make—for my sake, my husband's sake, and for our daughter's sake.

I (Hugh) saw my parents stay together even though I witnessed difficult times between them. While they didn't model an altogether healthy way of communicating (they simply didn't at times), they chose to stay together for the sake of the kids. And because marriage is forever. They did remain together—for 47 years, until my dad passed away at the age of 70. As I officiated at my dad's memorial service, I was able to look my mom in the eye—in front of all who knew and loved dad—and say, "Mom, you kept your vow 'till death do us part,' and for that I commend you." Her smile, in the midst of the grief she felt from having lost her life partner, showed us that it was, indeed, worth it.

We are determined to give ourselves and our daughter the gift of a marriage that lasts a lifetime. We want our Dana to see that marriage is forever. So hers will be, too. And not just *staying together* forever, but truly being in love, being with one's best friend, walking together, cultivating a closer connection…for the rest of our living days. That is our goal. We truly believe it is yours as well.

Taking the Next Step

Scripture tells us that with God, *all* things are possible. That's God's part—making the impossible possible. Our part is included in the Bible's description of love in 1 Corinthians 13:7: "[love] bears all things, believes all things, hopes all things, endures all things" (NASB). Did you catch that? Love bears, believes, hopes, and endures *all* things.

Within those words is the formula for a marriage that stands the test of time. Within those words of God is the key to achieving what might look impossible. The character of God plus the character of God's love within *you* equals an unstoppable, indivisible marriage.

Will you take to God all of the "impossibles" in your marriage? Will you give Him *all* of the disappointments and dashed dreams? Will you set at His feet all of the failures, unmet expectations, and wounds that have accumulated through the years and start over with an "all things are possible" trust in Him? Then add to that a "bear, believe, hope, and endure all things" type of love for your spouse. With that combination—God's power to do the impossible plus your God-given ability to love your partner as God would have you love him or her—nothing can divide you, debilitate you, or destroy you.

All things really *are* possible. Believe it—together.

—— Going the Extra Mile ——

1. Read the following passages together and list how they are an encouragement to your marriage:

   a. Philippians 4:13—

   b. Philippians 4:19—

   c. Romans 8:28—

   d. 2 Corinthians 5:17—

2. Start listing everything that would become broken or lost if you and your spouse split up. Are you really okay with that? Can you honestly say that you could live day to day with that kind of "collateral damage"?

3. Let's take a quick biblical inventory: God created everything you see, hear, taste, and touch—and He created it all out of nothing. He spoke, and it happened. Later He flooded the entire globe over a period of 40 days. Still later He separated a large body of water so a bunch of slaves He happened to particularly love could walk across without getting their feet wet. And still later, through His Son the Lord Jesus Christ, He raised people from the dead, multiplied some tilapia and matzo to feed thousands, and told a storm to "Just be quiet for now because I'm trying to teach a lesson here." Now, we dare you to ask yourself: Do you really think that the problems you and your spouse are having are beyond the aid of a God like that?

——Going the Distance Through Prayer——

God of our hearts and our marriage:

You truly are the God of the impossible. Throughout Scripture we read of all You did, against all odds, to preserve a people for Yourself and then to die for and redeem those people so You could live with them for an eternity. How fortunate we are to even be able to call You our Lord and Savior. And yet You still offer to us Your hand of protection, Your hand of deliverance, Your hand of help from day to day so we can live in communion with each other and with You.

We know by now that marriage is something that simply cannot survive without Your intervention and Your Spirit's intercession. How we need You to defeat the odds and help us not only survive, but thrive as a couple who is committed to staying together till death do us part. We truly believe You are the God of the impossible and that all things—no matter how big or unbearable they might look at the time—are possible through You. May our continued commitment to each other—even when the path looks impossible—be a witness to others of how big You really are.

When the Path
Leads You Home

Jesus answered, "I am the way and the truth and the
life. No one comes to the Father except through me."

JOHN 14:6

The old man reached out to help steady his wife as he opened the car door and helped her in. He then walked slowly around the back of the car to the driver's side and got in the car.

"That will be us someday," Hugh commented as we watched them and smiled. "Old as the hills, barely able to walk, and still shopping at Target together."

There's something special about growing old together. It's God's design for marriage.

Dick and Shirley, a couple in our church who just celebrated 58 years of marriage, are another husband and wife we hope to be like. It's so obvious they are best friends.

"I'm glad we appear to be best friends," Dick told us recently. "At our age it is probably easier to be best friends than it is to be wild, crazy, romantic, physical lovers."

But even in their late seventies they still share a spontaneous hug or a kiss, or a touch in passing. "We always end the day with 'I love you' and a hug," they said.

Dick and Shirley developed a closeness by relying on each other for most of their married life. And they've done that intentionally.

"By Shirley not driving and me not cooking, we have come to depend on each other and just work together," Dick said. The result? They go nearly everywhere together. And they've become best friends.

"Really, it goes back to just being dependent on one another. Over the years we've just enjoyed doing the simple, everyday stuff together. Recently we found ourselves in the supermarket on a Saturday evening. The thought occurred to us that Saturday night used to be date night or party night, and now we have progressed to buying groceries on Saturday night. But it's another together thing."

Cindi's Uncle Owen and Aunt Alice have taken the opposite approach.

"One of the things that has been beneficial to us, especially in retirement, is cross-training," Owen said. "It's something that's done in the military. It means to learn each other's jobs so if one of us is sick, injured, or needs extra help, then the other one can step right in and provide when needed."

"I've told him I think I should go first and that's why he should get into the kitchen," joked Alice, who is a few years older than Owen.

Dick and Shirley have learned to depend on each other. Owen and Alice have learned each other's jobs so they can each help each other. Two different philosophies, but with the same goal: togetherness.

Both couples admit that in their younger years, the closeness was more difficult to achieve because of the demands placed upon them by jobs, raising a family, church activities, and the pressures of everyday life.

Dick points out, "The end-of-the-day hug did not always happen in our early years. In those days, irritations were not quickly overcome. After Christ came into our lives (during our thirties), I can remember driving to church and being mad and not talking. However, we soon learned that by putting our Lord first we could not remain mad at each other. Upon leaving church all was well with the world. That happened many times in the early days."

Alice also recalls times when she and Owen weren't as gracious to each other as they are today.

"I can remember about a dozen times when we each needed our space," Alice recalls. "I would feel like going out and working in the yard."

"Now that's what we do every day—to be together!" Owen added. Owen also recalled other regrets: "When I was younger I didn't verbalize to Alice that I loved her or recognize how important it was for my wife to hear my love expressed. Now I realize how important it is, and I do it more often these days. I think a lot comes from the maturity that is gained through the years and learning to do things together. We go to the mall together now…shopping for something for her. I've learned a lot about things like that—about what she does—since I've retired."

Their daughter, Tami, says of her parents, "They've always been each other's strength in a way. I can't imagine either one of them without each other."

The younger years for Owen and Alice—and Dick and Shirley—weren't as intentional as their retirement years are. But they offer that to give us hope.

"Most of us older folks are quick to give advice to younger families about making the most of their time together," Dick said. "But the reason is so that hopefully they will not make the same mistakes we made. Once the days, weeks, months, and years are gone, you cannot retrieve them and have a do-over." They are now living with the reality of that. And making the most of the days they have left—together.

The stories are the same, aren't they? Kids come. Full-time jobs press in. The schedules get tight. Hassles and the routines of everyday life take over. Yet once these couples reach their golden years together, the house is quiet and they have each other. Perhaps it is the wisdom that age brings or the knowledge that time is ticking away and they are getting older and a little more feeble that makes them more appreciative of the time they still have together.

We tell you these things so you won't lose hope. So you will look at a couple in their eighties who are still in love and say, "That will be us someday." So you will understand that if your marriage is in one of those more difficult stages right now, that it does get easier as time goes on. Marriage is about transitions. It is about walking together through the stages of life and persevering—and when you do, the last stage will be a precious, meaningful, intimate stage for both of you.

Couples who invest now in their golden years together—through date nights, taking the time to connect, walking together through this book and others—are placing a deposit into the account of their golden years that they will be able to draw from and live off of later.

"People give up on their marriages too early," said Midge, who discovered how very much she and Ray had in common after all when they built their house together. "But you need to wait and get through those difficult times and then everything gets so much easier. It *does* get easier, if you are patient." Midge said commitment keeps you battling through the tough years and then a love and respect for your partner takes you sailing through those golden years.

That's good to know for those of you still in the transitional years during which your commitment seems like it is being put to the test daily. You may find there are days when you truly don't like each other. But God's continual shaping of your heart, through a constant effort of walking together, will get you to the place where you can close out life with your best friend at your side.

So it was bittersweet as I (Cindi) talked with June about a year after she lost her beloved Bill to bone cancer. Forty-nine years together, and a part of her is now gone. Yet she stands strong and lives on because of a foundation that was built years ago. As much as she and Bill loved each other and enjoyed being together, they each looked to God as their first love. So as much as June misses Bill today, she continues to live for God—the Lover of her soul—knowing one day she will again be with the *two* greatest loves of her life.

June is still investing in the lives of her children, grandchildren, and great-grandchildren. She is actively involved at her church and she keeps in touch with friends, seeing life as a gift. June is able to go on, though, because Bill was her husband, not her god.

A marriage in which the spouses just focus on each other is not healthy. A husband worshipping his wife and vice versa is not the answer. It is a focus on God that draws two people together and helps them make it through the storms of life. Then when one goes home, the other can follow in God's timing without feeling devastation or despair.

Our walk with God and our partner here on earth is practice for the sweet walk of fellowship we will one day enjoy when we walk the streets of gold with our Maker.

Taking the Next Step

So what will *you* do from this point onward to ensure that your connection will last a lifetime? We have seen from experience—and heard from the rich examples of couples in this book—that it all comes down to these three principles:

Lay your foundation—Make sure it is God you both are living for first, and not each other. Second Timothy 2:19 tells us "the firm foundation of God stands."[38] A love for and commitment to God will enable you to learn of His unconditional love for you, which then teaches you how to unconditionally love your spouse and others. That is the only kind of love that lasts forever. Eternal, endless love—the kind God has for us—is what fuels our love for each other here on this earth. The Bible tells us, "This is how we know what love is: Jesus Christ laid down his life for us. And we ought to lay down our lives for our brothers" (1 John 3:16). We are also told, "We love because he first loved us" (1 John 4:19). Without a proper knowledge and experience of God's love for us, we cannot possibly know how to love our husband or wife.

Live with the knowledge that your days are numbered—In Psalm 90:12, Moses sang a prayer that offers us insight on how to live more wisely: "Teach us to number our days aright, that we may gain a heart of wisdom." If we would approach life knowing that our days are numbered, we would be more careful how we lived and loved, what we said to each other, and which opportunities we let slip away. In The Message, that verse reads, "Oh! Teach us to live well! Teach us to live wisely and well!" Your days with your spouse *are* numbered here on earth.

Seek God's wisdom to live those days wisely—as if each one was your last.

Leave a legacy—We talked about having a mission for your marriage. If that mission is truly empowered by God's Spirit, it will live on after you are gone. Whether you are investing in others' lives, building the kingdom of God, or simply teaching your children—or grandchildren—to pray, you are leaving a legacy that will live on after you and your spouse go home to the Lord. Maybe you're thinking, *What kind of legacy can we possibly leave?* Think of the people who have come in and gone out of your lives. Do you ever have the chance to impact another couple positively? Do you have children who are seeing your marriage work? Those things right there, our friends, are the beginning of a legacy.

Owen and Alice. Dick and Shirley. The elderly, feeble couple in the Target parking lot. Best of friends. Companions for life. Each of them unable to fathom life on earth with anyone else at their side. Each hoping to reach heaven's gates together because they can't imagine going on in life without the other by their side. One can only hope that when God calls them home, He'll call them home together.

Owen and Alice. Dick and Shirley. Each living first for God, each numbering their days, and each leaving a legacy as we read about their togetherness.

Yes, that's what we want our marriage to look like someday. And by God's grace we'll get there…and so will *you*.

—— Going the Extra Mile ——

Here are some ways for you to consider and build your legacy for your children, grandchildren, and others:

1. Dream a little of what you'd like your legacy to be, long after you both have left this earth. Just by dreaming it together, you are expanding your vision of what God can do through your lives and marriage.

2. Why not take the time now to write out a letter to each other as if you each only had a month left to live? What would you say to each other that you haven't said in a while? What have you always wished you could have done together? Say what you need to say, and say it now.

3. Use the following passages as a guide for how to pray about passing on a legacy to the next generation: Psalm 37:25, Proverbs 13:22a, 2 Timothy 1:5, Titus 2:2-5, 1 John 2:12-14.

——Going the Distance Through Prayer——

Lord Jesus, how we long to close out our years side by side, together, with the one You have given us to live life at our side. We truly want our journey to be one that we enjoyed and that You were pleased with. We want it to be a journey others will continue to talk about simply because they remember how we were each other's best friend. Help us to continue to lay a foundation that will never crumble by putting You first in our hearts. Help us to number our days so we will live wisely and not pass up opportunities we might never get back. And help us to leave a legacy so all will know what You were able to accomplish in and through us.

You have said in Your Word that You are the way, the truth, and the life. Be the way…that leads us home safely to You. Be the truth in our marriage when nothing else makes sense. Be the life that we live fully and uprightly for Your glory. May we ever keep our eyes on You, the way, the path—the Only One who can truly lead us all the way home…together.

Notes

1. Genesis 2:18.
2. John and Stasi Eldredge, *Love and War* (New York: Doubleday, 2010), p. 15.
3. Luke 22:42 NKJV.
4. This prayer paraphrases 1 Corinthians 13:4-8 as stated in The Message.
5. 1 Corinthians 13:8.
6. Eldredge, *Love and War,* p. 14.
7. Genesis 5:22-24.
8. This account is found in Luke 24:13-35.
9. The Message.
10. You can find Freedom in Christ resources at www.freedominchrist.com.
11. For more information on the Weekend to Remember marriage conference, go to www.familylife.com.
12. Robert Jeffress, *Say Goodye to Regret* (Sisters, OR: Multnomah Publishers, 1998), p. 42.
13. Psalm 90:12 MSG.
14. The book that sparked the conversation was *When Women Walk Alone* (Eugene, OR: Harvest House, 2002).
15. This article, "The Secret to a Lasting Marriage," is based on Dennis Rainey's book by the same title and was found in "The Family Room Archives" at www.familylife.com.
16. Philippians 2:2 NASB.
17. In Leviticus 27:30-33, a tithe was required by the Israelites to sustain the priests' livelihood.
18. Matthew 7:9-11; James 1:17.
19. Kay Warren, *Dangerous Surrender* (Grand Rapids: Zondervan, 2007), p. 22.
20. NASB.
21. Dennis Rainey, "Thirty Ways to Love Your Lover," an article that appeared on www.familylife.com based on Dennis and Barbara Rainey's book *Rekindling the Romance* (Nashville: Thomas Nelson, 2004).
22. 1 John 3:18.
23. 1 Thessalonians 5:18.
24. MSG, emphasis in original.
25. NASB.
26. Kathi Lipp, *The Marriage Project: 21 Days to More Love and Laughter* (Eugene, OR: Harvest House, 2009). For more information on this book and *The Husband Project,* see www.projectsforthesoul.com.
27. 1 Corinthians 13:7 NASB.
28. Philippians 4:6-7 NLT.
29. NLT.
30. NASB.
31. NIV.
32. We are told to think on the characteristics listed in Philippians 4:8. Anything that contradicts these characteristics comes not from God, but from our enemy.
33. Ecclesiastes 4:12b.
34. John 11:25.
35. In Exodus 15:22-26, God revealed Himself as Jehovah Rapha (The LORD who heals).
36. Matthew 19:26.
37. John and Stasi Eldredge, *Love and War,* p. 207.
38. NASB.

Other Books by Cindi McMenamin

When Women Walk Alone

Whether you feel alone from being single, facing challenging life situations, or from being the spiritual head of your household, discover practical steps to finding support, transforming loneliness into spiritual growth, and turning your alone times into life-changing encounters with God.

Letting God Meet Your Emotional Needs

Discover true intimacy with God in this book that shows how to draw closer to the lover of your soul and find that He can, indeed, meet your deepest emotional needs.

Women on the Edge

Every woman has times when she feels as if she's unappreciated, unsupported, and weary. Will you let the resulting frustration drive you away from God, or closer to Him? Cindi shares how you can thrive even in the hard times.

When Women Walk Alone: A 31-Day Devotional Companion

Feeling overwhelmed? Frustrated? Alone? God is at your side, ready to speak to your heart. He knows how you feel and longs to help—whether you are in need of guidance, encouragement, or comfort. Experience God's presence at all times with the help of this 31-day devotional companion.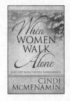

When a Woman Discovers Her Dream

It's never too late to discover and live out your dreams in life. Explore God's purpose for you, and make greater use of your uniqueness and special gifts.

When Women Long for Rest

When Woman Long for Rest is an invitation to find your quiet place at God's feet—a place where you can listen to Him, open your heart to Him, and experience true rest.

An Invitation to Write

How has this book helped you and your spouse toward a closer connection? Hugh and Cindi would love to hear from you and know how you've been ministered to or encouraged through their writing. You can contact them online at Cindispeaks@msn.com or write to:

Hugh and Cindi McMenamin
c/o Harvest House Publishers
990 Owen Loop North
Eugene, OR 97402-9173

If you would like Hugh and Cindi to speak to your group, you may contact them and receive more information about their speaking ministry at:

www.StrengthForTheSoul.com